SUNDERLAND COLLEGE

0002588

D0348022

Sunderland College

Bede/Headways Learning Centre

This book is due for return on or before the last date shown below
Please be aware that sanctions are applied for overdue items
Renew online via Moodle
Renew by phone: call 5116344

Author MACKRELL J.

Class 792.809   Location Code   D

21 DAY LOAN

OUT OF LINE

THE STORY OF
BRITISH NEW DANCE

Judith Mackrell

CITY OF
LEARNING
CENTRE
SUNDERLAND COLLEGE

DANCE BOOKS

CITY OF SUNDERLAND COLLEGE LEARNING CENTRE		£ 12·50·
ORDER NUMBER	LS\30983	
DATE OF ACCESSION	1.2009	
ACCESSION NUMBER	0002588	
RECOMMENDED BY	Emma Kennedan.	

First published in 1992 by Dance Books Ltd

© Judith Mackrell 1992

ISBN 1 85273 038 2

Designed by Sanjoy Roy.

A CIP catalogue record of this book is available from the
British Library.

Contents

Illustrations

Author's Note

This book is a history of new British dance from the late 1960s onwards: the story of how dancers and choreographers began to make work independently of the large established dance companies, and of the kind of work they made. At the centre of this story is, of course, the rise of the New Dance movement, which was crucial in the development of independent dance. But it must be remembered that there has been a lot of new and independent work which is not actually a part of that movement – in terms either of its style or of its ideas. So throughout the book I have tried to keep a clear distinction between New Dance as a movement, new dance as a very general term, and *New Dance* the magazine through which many of the ideas associated with New Dance were publicised.

In describing the work of choreographers and companies during this period I have tried to use a variety of sources and opinions and I have always made it obvious where these come from; where no source is cited, quotations are from unpublished interviews with myself. When a description or a judgement is not attributed to anyone else, it is mine, and it is of course a personal one.

My thanks to Jan Murray, Joan White, Chris de Marigny, and the New Dance collective; above all to the people about whom this book is written – the people who made the independent dance scene happen.

What is New Dance?

New Dance is a mini-revolution which started over twenty years ago on the fringes of the British dance scene. It is a revolution which has been partly about choreographic experiment and partly about altering the way people think about dance. Like most revolutions it has never been organised by a single body of people, nor has it had a strictly defined aim. It is a movement which has been fuelled by a range of political and artistic ideas, all of which have helped to shape the dance scene as we know it today.

An important key to understanding New Dance has always been its openness to a wide range of influences and ideas. No single ideology and no single approach to choreography has dominated the movement. Fergus Early, who has been involved with New Dance from its beginnings, has argued emphatically that 'style' is actually 'useless as a definition of New Dance':

> New Dance is not:
> baggy trousers, rolling about, chinese shoes, contact improvisation, ballet to rock music, release work, image work, outside performances, post-modern dance, martial arts, self-indulgence, American, non-narrative . . .

> New Dance does not exclude:
> formal choreography, tap, ballet class, baggy trousers, rolling about, chinese shoes, jazz shoes, no shoes, army boots, self-indulgence, contact improvisation, rock music, virtuosity, stillness, narrative . . .

In conclusion Early says:

> The one and only essential concept to New Dance is Liberation.
> (Paper for the Chisenhale/NODM weekend to celebrate New Dance, May 1986)

But if New Dance is about liberation, what has it tried to liberate itself from? To understand what Early means we not only have to know what New Dance has attempted to achieve but also to understand the limiting conditions from which it has tried to escape.

Until the early 1960s very few people in Britain had seen, or knew about modern dance, and even fewer knew about the experimental 'post-modern' scene (see Glossary) that was starting up in America. 'Serious' dance was still equated with ballet, and the dance world was dominated by long-established traditions. For instance, most professional dancers were expected to have at least ten years' classical training before they appeared on stage, while choreographers were expected to have worked inside a company for some time before creating their own works. There were very few non-classical dance companies, and although a few smaller ballet companies existed alongside the two Royal Ballet companies, it was rare for dancers and choreographers to work independently of any company at all.

The opportunities for non-professionals to do any kind of dance were also limited. There were amateur folk groups around, and adults might also go to ballroom dancing or to some kind of keep-fit class. Children who did not attend ballet, tap or stage dance classes might do a folk or a 'music and movement' style of dance class at school. There was also a strong interest in European modern dance within certain schools and educational bodies, influenced by the Hungarian choreographer and dance researcher Rudolf Laban. But in general, dance was looked at with deep suspicion by the British public – it was something that only professionals did, in ballets, pantomimes or musicals.

Many things changed this situation, the most important of which was the formation of the two big modern dance companies, London Contemporary Dance Theatre and Ballet Rambert, in the late 1960s. But the more radical alternatives to the old systems were created by people within the New Dance movement, both in the ways that they made their choreography, and in the kinds of arguments they tried to put into practice.

While it is dangerous to try and identify the movement as a single group with a single philosophy, some of the most important ideas which the New Dance movement has fought to establish are as follows:

(1) Dance takes many forms, all of which should be treated as seriously as ballet. Post-modern dance, folk dance, break dance, Afro-Caribbean and Indian dance, even techniques developed by individual dancers, are all legitimate and interesting aspects of dance.

(2) Dancers and choreographers must be able to produce and perform whatever kind of dance they want, and should be free to work outside established companies.

(3) Dance is not just a highly specialised profession: it is a basic part of living, and anyone should be encouraged to do it, no matter what age, shape or colour they are.

(4) Dance should not be divorced from the real world. Dancers should be encouraged to think about the politics and economics of their situation, and choreographers should not be scared of presenting work that makes some kind of statement about society.

(5) Dancers and choreographers should be given equal status and equal funding as artists working in other forms.

This book is about the individuals and the companies who either helped to initiate the New Dance movement or were influenced by it. It is about the ideas and the events which shaped the course of the movement, about the kinds of changes which it has brought about, and about the way that these changes have become an integral part of British dance today.

History of the Movement

Signs of change

In 1963, Teresa Early founded an organisation called Ballet-makers Ltd, which took an important first step in showing how dancers and choreographers could organise themselves independently of the established companies. Early (Fergus's sister) had been to ballet classes for much of her life but wasn't physically suited to being a professional classical dancer. This did not stop her from wanting to choreograph and dance however, and she started to look for ways in which she could do so on her own. This meant finding other dancers, as well as musicians, designers, a space to rehearse in and a space where they could perform.

So she got together a group of dancers and choreographers who shared her frustrations, charged a yearly membership fee of a guinea, borrowed £20, and set up Balletmakers Ltd as a registered company. Various halls were rented to provide space for rehearsals, classes and workshops and the group's programme included weekly classes in dance composition, informal showings of work, and yearly performances at the Lyric, Hammersmith or Richmond Theatres.

Right from the beginning Balletmakers worked on an open-door policy, which meant that anyone could join. The members included not only isolated individuals like Early herself, but also dancers and choreographers from The Royal Ballet and Ballet Rambert, since even for privileged members of large companies the opportunities to experiment with new work were very limited.

Initially most of the work was classically based, and also very ambitious. Fergus Early, who was closely involved with the group, remembers an early piece that lasted twenty minutes and used a full symphony orchestra drawn from London's music colleges. But by the mid-1960s a few classes were held in modern dance technique, and Balletmakers' performances began to show a strong modern dance influence. There was no clash between classical and modern work however, because Teresa Early believed, like many of those who were later associated with New Dance, that dance embraces many forms:

> We believed that dance was one thing, in contrast to the sacred prejudices of each school (ballet is so artificial/modern dance is bad for the knees ankles buttocks/folk is quaint my dear but not art . . .) and that good of any kind was good. Any style of work might have, and had, a place on our programmes.
>
> (T. Early: 'What Balletmakers Was',
> *New Dance* No. 2, 1976, pp. 16–17)

In 1967, when London Contemporary Dance Theatre was in its formative stages, it used the annual Balletmakers performance to present some of its work – including Robert North's first piece of choreography. There was, however, surprisingly little recognition in the dance world of how important Balletmakers was, or how important it could have become, given greater encouragement. Teresa Early remembers that the first press reviews were hostile, because critics didn't like the fact that they were seeing work which was often at an early stage of development. In the article quoted above she writes: 'the thought that what they were viewing was not the end but the beginning of a process did not seem to occur to any of them'.

Though reactions improved a little, no significant financial support was ever given to the group. Choreographers and dancers alike were working under very limiting conditions, and there was no way that Balletmakers could effectively foster new talent.

But even if the group did not produce outstanding or innovative work, it was still of real importance. The fact that it was a collective organisation which gave people the freedom to create their own work was to prove an invaluable example for future groups to follow.

During the late 1950s and early 1960s British society started to become more liberal and open-minded, and ideas about art began to change. The composer Cornelius Cardew, for example, wrote radical new music that made little use of conventional instruments and allowed the musicians to decide when they would start (and stop) playing. An exhibition in London's Whitechapel Gallery in 1956 called 'This is Tomorrow' marked the beginnings of the pop art movement in Britain – a style which often used advertising or comic strip images and made no pretensions to being high art. The first performance of Beckett's *Waiting for Godot* in 1955 sparked off the Theatre of the Absurd movement – in which plays no longer followed a logical plot, and strange ritualised actions often became a substitute for the text. French novelists like Alain Robbe-Grillet (who wrote novels without plots and characters) and American poets like Alan Ginsberg (who wrote poems using slang) encouraged British writers like B. S. Johnson and Adrian Mitchell to experiment with language. And of course pop music (the Beatles, the Rolling Stones, and others) changed the way in which a younger generation saw itself. A succession of rapidly changing street fashions (Beatle-cuts, long hair, drainpipes, mini-skirts, flares, kaftans etc.) challenged previous ideas of respectability and style, and suddenly it became understood that everyone under thirty would criticise the politics and life-style of their parents.

The 1960s was also a time of economic expansion in Britain. People had money to spend on clothes, records and going to the theatre – and the more they demanded novelty, the more the arts provided it for them. Just as importantly, there was a large increase in the amount of public spending on the arts, and many experimental projects that could not have survived in a purely commercial context were given support.

These developments inevitably led to a change in attitudes towards dance. When Martha Graham first performed in London in 1954, most of the audience were completely bewildered by her work. As far as many people were concerned, it was not ballet so it could not be dance, and only a few grasped the importance of what they saw. However, when Graham returned to Edinburgh and London in 1963, audiences were ecstatic, and soon afterwards showed similar enthusiasm for Merce Cunningham and Paul Taylor.

Suddenly it looked as though Britain was ready for modern dance, and in 1966 Robin Howard (a London businessman and devotee of Graham) decided to establish a school where modern dance could be taught, as well as a company which could perform it. The London School of Contemporary Dance actually started out as a series of moveable classes, but it soon found a permanent home at The Place (initially called the Artists' Place). The company, which was founded in 1967, was called London Contemporary Dance Theatre.

It was from The Place that most of the original energy for British modern dance, and later New Dance, was to spring. Today, the school is a relatively formal institution, with strict standards of entry and an inherited commitment to Graham-derived technique in its teaching. But in the 1960s it was open to any kind of influence. Many of its earliest students, for example, had little dance training, and came from completely different disciplines – Richard Alston and Siobhan Davies were originally art students, while Sally Potter was a film-maker – and their experience of other art forms contributed to some of their more revolutionary ideas about choreography. Other students, like Jacky Lansley and Fergus Early, were trained ballet dancers who were searching for alternative approaches to dance.

During the early years, when a kind of creative anarchy ruled at The Place, these alternatives were very much on offer. A variety of styles were taught by visiting teachers, including Cunningham, Limón and Nikolais techniques. There were regular workshops in which dancers, musicians, designers, actors and theatre directors all participated (some of which were open to non-students as well) and there were many opportunities for the students to make and show their own choreography (the school believed that students should be trained as creative dance artists, not just as dance technicians). Just as the early students were under no pressure to conform to a particular type of dancer, so they were free to create their own style of choreography. People were suddenly inventing their own routes into dance, like the three choreographers whose early experiences at The Place are discussed below.

Richard Alston

Alston's initial interest in dance was sparked by his fascination with the work of Sophie Fedorovitch, a stage designer who worked closely with Frederick Ashton at The Royal Ballet. He started watching ballet regularly, and it was during a performance of *La Fille mal gardée* that he realised he wanted to make dances rather than paint pictures. He started by taking ballet classes. But

7

knowing that he was far too late to begin classical training, and sensing the excitement coming from The Place, he entered the London School of Contemporary Dance in 1967.

At that point his experience of modern dance was limited, though he had seen Graham, and in 1966 had gone to watch Cunningham with some other art students. His interest in the latter was mostly aroused by the painters with whom Cunningham was collaborating (like Robert Rauschenberg) and he now confesses that he couldn't make head or tail of the choreography. (Later, Cunningham was to become a very important influence on Alston's work.)

Alston remembers The Place at that time as:

> . . . very erratically organised, which allowed for a lot of free-dom. There were some very odd strange students, people like Sally Potter who has now gone back into making films, people who have ended up making performance work [see Glossary]. There was a great interest in alternative work then, before the pressure to get established encouraged a more conformist approach.
>
> I remember Meredith Monk [see Glossary] came in 1972 and did a vast great piece with hundreds of students doing things all round the building . . . you kind of found them as you went around . . . and then she did a solo performance of *Education of the Girl Child* in the theatre. After that she went up to Liverpool and did a huge piece called *Vessel* with ele-phants and crowds of Liverpudlian kids up and down the streets, it was great.
>
> (Interview with author, 1985)

Right from the beginning, Alston was more interested in making dance than in performing it, and he produced his first piece, *Transit*, for a workshop in 1968. In his third year at The Place he organised a group of advanced students (including Siobhan Davies) to perform demonstration programmes at schools and colleges, in which all the works shown were his own. (The interest in new music, which was to become an important feature of his choreography, could already be seen in his choice of composers such as Cage, Stockhausen and Michael Finnissy.)

The following year Alston taught a course in experimental

Tuesday — Thursday — Saturday

"JUICE" (1969)

Cast in order of appearance:

King:	Mark Monstermaker
Fiddler:	Haan
Light:	Madeline Slovenz
~~Red~~ People:	Lanny Harrison
Red	Meredith Monk
	Ping Chong
	John Smead
	Daniel Ira Sverdlik
Woman by Rock:	Monica Mosley
Hostess:	Linn Varney
Tableaux:	Coco Pekelis
	Gerry Kelter
	Mark Monstermaker
	Blondell Cummings
	Students from THE PLACE

Music by Meredith Monk ℗ 1969

Wednesday — Friday

"EDUCATION OF THE GIRLCHILD" (1972)

Meredith Monk

INTERVAL

"RAW RECITAL" (1970)

Meredith Monk   Ping Chong

Music by Meredith Monk ℗ 1969-72
Monk/3 Coughs Music Co.

*Music from this concert is recorded on "Key: an album of Invisible Theatre"
(Increase Records). Copies can be obtained at the theatre or by mail order
to:*   *Increase Records,*
                 931 N. La Cienega Blvd.,
                 Los Angeles,
                 California,
                 U.S.A.

Programme of Meredith Monk's performance at The Place Theatre, 1972.

9

composition at The Place, by which time some of his work had been taken into the repertory of London Contemporary Dance Theatre (*Something to Do* was performed in 1970, *Nowhere Slowly* in 1971; *Cold* – a reworking of Act II of *Giselle* with the original music by Adolphe Adam – and *Tiger Balm* appeared in the same season in 1972).

If Alston had chosen to stay with London Contemporary Dance Theatre he would have been given every opportunity to choreograph for the company. His talent was recognised, and British modern choreographers were still thin on the ground. But Alston wanted to move on.

To begin with he wasn't particularly interested in the Graham technique which formed the basis of the company's style. The movement itself was not to his taste, and even more importantly, he disliked Graham's idea that dance had to express emotion. Perhaps because of his art school training he was more interested in the shape and the line of movement, in its formal rather than its dramatic qualities. He also wanted to take risks in his work, to experiment with new kinds of movement and different ways of performing, and this did not fit in with London Contemporary Dance Theatre's determination to appeal to large audiences.

> I found the company's audience-seeking syndrome unacceptable. They told me that they were looking for a middle-class audience with money to spend at the theatre, so they didn't want to do anything too shocking. Well, at twenty-one that was enough to make me see red.
>
> There was some grant from the Gulbenkian [Foundation] which had just started, and Robin Howard wanted to send me to New York for a year and come back full of inspiration and energy to choreograph things for London Contemporary. But I decided that I just wanted to stay over here and work with a small group of people.
>
> So in 1972 I took three other dancers from The Place who I thought were really interesting and who weren't going to join the company, Jacky Lansley, Christopher Banner and Wendy Levett, and I formed Strider.
>
> (Interview with author, 1985)

Vessel (1971) choreographed by Meredith Monk.

Jacky Lansley

Jacky Lansley went to dance school from a very young age where she was taught ballet and tap, as well as acting and singing. (She is certain that the variety in her early training inspired her to use so many different styles of dance and performance in her later choreography.) At the age of sixteen she went to The Royal Ballet School and soon afterwards joined The Royal Ballet.

Lansley regards her life in The Royal Ballet as a crucial part of her training: 'It gave me a bedrock of professionalism, learning what it's like to pick things up quickly, to understand the rehearsal process, to cope with the slog'. But she is very critical of the kind of pressure to conform to a particular physical image, and the pressure to rise up the company hierarchy. When she had a serious injury Lansley became very conscious of how demanding and unsettling these pressures were, and realised that she had to leave:

> I didn't get any support from anyone during the time I was injured and I was suddenly aware of all these other young

11

women waiting to take my place. I realised I was completely dispensable so I decided not to just cope with it, but explode out of it and move on. It was a very radical step for me, to leave something like The Royal Ballet, but I'm glad I did it.

After a year or so I got a grant and went to The Place as a student. It was a wonderful time for me. The Place was very flexible then, and I met a very interesting mix of people, all doing interesting work. I really got engrossed in the whole process of choreography, rather than getting involved in Graham, a technique which I was quite critical of – I thought it was physically quite destructive.

I also got involved with Richard Alston and Strider, which you could say was the first post-modern dance group in this country. I choreographed a piece for the first show at the ICA [Institute of Contemporary Arts] called *Halfway to Paradise* [1972]. I was very influenced by 'performance art' and by the work I'd seen by Meredith Monk.

Sally [Potter] had been making films since the age of sixteen and I was very interested by her ideas. But the biggest thing that influenced me was feminism [see Glossary]. I was really ripe for that big explosion of feminist thought in the early 1970s and I really got into it. One of central themes in all the work I did was looking at roles and images of women.

I worked with Strider for a year until I began to feel that I was being used as a performer again, even though I was also making work, so I went back to The Place for another year and made heaps and heaps of pieces for workshop performances. Sally and I worked together a lot and after a year we formed Limited Dance Company, just the two of us.

(Interview with author, 1985)

Fergus Early

As a young child Fergus Early took classes in ballet, tap, national and Greek dance, and at the age of ten went to The Royal Ballet School. His favourite classes were in English folk dance, a style that is still a strong influence on his choreography. In 1964 he joined the touring company of The Royal Ballet, and later on worked closely with Ballet for All (a touring educational group associated with the company) which gave him the opportunity he was looking for to choreograph. By 1971 he was working

```
TIGER BALM - for Christopher Banner

choreography          Richard Alston
music                 Tiger Balm by Anna Lockwood
lighting              Charles Paton

dancers (18th,21st,22nd) Robert North    Siobhan Davies
                         Larrio Ekson    Linda Gibbs
                         Xenia Hribar    Noemi Lapzeson

        (28th,29th,6th ) Micha Bergose   Celeste Dandeker
                         Catherine Harrison  Paula Lansley
                         Eva Lundqvist.  Ross McKim

"I took the idea and the structure of this piece from the sounds,
which were already completed.  They were so strong that I tried
to make everything as simple, as pared down as possible, absorb-
ing some of the feeling of those sounds - such as animal fear
and a somnolent calm."  Richard Alston


TREEO

choreography          Xenia Hribar
music                 Alastair Leonard (piano)
lighting              Michael Alston

dancers               Stephen Barker   Paula Lansley   Namron

"This dance grew from an idea that was completely serious.
There was a tree, a girl and an older man - then, as usually
happens to me, the whole thing took its own course and came out
funny.  It is about Eva, as I know her best - and I do feel
rather sorry for her."  Xenia Hribar

                        ********

The London CONTEMPORARY DANCE THEATRE gratefully acknowledges
the financial assistance it receives from the Arts Council of
Great Britain, the Greater London Council and the London
Borough of Camden.
```

London Contemporary Dance Theatre programme, featuring Richard Alston's early work *Tiger Balm* (1972).

full-time with Ballet for All – helping to put shows together which involved actors, musicians and dancers – and in particular working with the dance historian and choreographer Mary Skeaping, whose task was to recreate old ballets. (All of this work links up with Early's later choreography which has often included dialogue, and in many cases has reworked old ballets from a modern perspective.)

Throughout this period, Early was also involved with Balletmakers. This gave him other opportunities to choreograph,

13

and also, through the group's classes and workshops, his first introduction to modern dance – 'I remember my sister doing a spoof Cunningham piece called *Merce or Worse*.'

When Early started to watch modern dance performances, he remembers being 'bowled over by Cunningham. I couldn't believe that dancers could look like that, that they could be all sorts of weird shapes and sizes and that they could do all those strange things. I didn't really like Graham's choreography much. I prefer it more now.' Further contact with modern dance came when Ballet For All worked with the Graham company in 1965 on a joint project which compared ballet with modern dance. And all of this meant that Early was not, like so many of his contemporaries, 'walled up in ballet'. He saw that 'ballet was very limited' and began to understand how difficult it would be for him to choreograph the kind of work that interested him if he stayed in a ballet company.

In 1970–71 I went to see [Kenneth] MacMillan and asked him what the prospects were for choreographing with the company. I'd done all this work for Ballet for All, as well as a piece for The Royal Ballet Choreographic Group which was called *The Pig and the Panther*. It was a cartoon kind of piece about a boxing match between a black panther and a pig for the heavyweight championship of the world – it was the time of the Black Panther movement – but they weren't impressed by this. MacMillan said he wanted to see if I could choreograph steps, they weren't interested in ideas. That was more or less the point when I knew for sure that it wasn't it.

I applied for a Gulbenkian Dance Award which had just started up, went to The Place for a year, and stayed on as a teacher for two years. That was the most important time for me. It was all pretty disorganised, and it was nice to teach ballet because it was very marginal on the curriculum. There were lots of open workshops for people outside as well as students and company workshops. And there were a lot of interesting mature students. I was able to do a lot of work in a very supportive situation.

There's no question that it all began at The Place, there was nowhere else, though towards the end it became much tighter, with auditions and a much stricter emphasis on Graham.

Looking back I can see my whole career in terms of thinking about spaces – Balletmakers, The Place, X6, Chisenhale, it's all been about setting up contexts that didn't previously exist in order for dancers and choreographers to work. Actual physical spaces, and time and organisation. Dance can't happen without those.

(Interview with author, 1985)

The first companies

There were too many ideas and too many students at The Place for it to function simply as a training ground for London Contemporary Dance Theatre, and very soon individuals began to form their own small dance groups and explore their own approaches to choreography. An avant-garde fringe was thus quick to develop, even though modern dance had only been established for a few years in this country.

Moving Being

Moving Being was not exactly a dance company (although movement played a strong part in its productions) nor did it strictly originate from The Place (though many of its early members were trained there and for a time it used The Place as its base). What makes it important to the history of New Dance is that like many of the independent dance groups which followed, it was set up to fill a vacuum. Its founder, Geoff Moore, had a vision of a multi-media theatre that no other company was exploring, and he formed his own group to pursue it.

Geoff Moore was an art student, stage manager and self-taught choreographer. He wanted to create a form of theatre using elements from different art forms, that was not restricted by traditional labels like dance or drama. So in 1968 he got together a group of dancers, actors, designers, film-makers, lighting people and costume-makers who could pool their creative ideas. The breadth of the company's interests is suggested by a note written in the programme for *The Real Life Attempt* (1973):

[The work's ideas are] to do with painting and the power of

15

the visual image, theatre and the 'presence' of live performance, film, music, newspaper reports, dancing and 'natural'
movement, science, popular culture, poetry, psychology,
information of all sorts about people and events.

Moving Being hit exactly the right note for the experimental
mood of the late 1960s, and appealed to a wide audience by cut-
ting across so many different disciplines. The company was initially sponsored by the ICA in London, and for three years it was
based at The Place. But in 1972 it set up a permanent base in
Cardiff with support from the Welsh Arts Council and Chapter
Arts Centre.

At the beginning the work tended to fall into separate sections
– each one highlighting dance, drama or visual effects – but they
tried, increasingly, to unify the different forms. In 1971 they
started work on a trilogy called *The Real Life Attempt* in which
each separate show (*Signs*, *Angels* and *Sun*) was a genuinely
mixed-media event. *Sun* (1972) was about the spiritual collapse
of the Western world, and to express this theme Moore brought
together fragments from an extraordinary range of writers and
composers. The text included quotations from Norman O.
Brown, R. D. Laing, Freud, Pete Townshend, Germaine Greer
and James Joyce, and there was taped music by The Beach Boys,
Mahler, Frank Zappa and Irving Berlin. Live music came from
Cherie Morello and Duke Box. In addition there were film
sequences by John Carter, plus complex lighting and projection
designs by Peter Mumford and costumes by Pamela Moore. The
whole thing was choreographed and directed by Geoff Moore
himself, with performances by John Carter, Chris Dawber,
Catherine Harrison, Ritva Lehtinen, Bernard Living and Pamela
Moore. The *Western Mail* described the show as follows:

> From oriental dances and the reflective mood of the first part
> of the work, we move . . . to an urgent need to face up to the
> spectre of death. Passages from Freud and Joyce wrestle with
> film of crashing cars and bombing raids; we sense ourselves to
> be trapped in the insane frenzy and artificiality of this life. At
> times, despite the pop idiom, one felt in the presence of the
> medieval dance of death as danced in the halls of Bedlam.
>
> (Programme for *The Real Life Attempt*, July 1973)

	TEXT:	NORMAN O. BROWN
		MICHAEL McCLURE
JOHN CARTER		SIMONE WEIL
CHRIS DAWBER *(helen c personal)*		R.D. LAING
CATHERINE HARRISON *(opening girl)*		MICHAEL ALLABY
RITVA LEHTINEN		ETIENNE LALOU
BERNARD LIVING		MARSHALL McCLUHAN
PAMELA MOORE *(with mike)*		SIGMUND FREUD
Setting Lighting Projection		PETE TOWNSHEND
PETER MUMFORD		GERMAINE GREER
Film		JAMES JOYCE
JOHN CARTER	MUSIC:	TERRY RILEY
Costumes		ROBIN WILLIAMSON
PAMELA MOORE		IVAN PAWLE
Live Music		LOS CALCHAKIS
CHERIE MORELLO		HOF-UND BANJAR-MUSIK
DUKE BOX		THE BEACH BOYS
Text and Sound Assemblage		THE INCREDIBLE STRING BAND
Choreography and Direction		JONATHEN KING
GEOFF MOORE		GUSTAV MAHLER
		IRVING BERLIN
		FRANK ZAPPA

There will be an interval of 15 minutes

Moving Being programme for *Sun* (1972).

Reviews were often glowing. In the same programme the critic from the *Observer* was quoted as follows:

Moore has devised a form of total theatre that is stimulating, vital and beautiful. He uses dancers who can act, sounds that can dance and light that can do almost anything.

And Jan Murray noted in a *Time Out* review in 1977 (quoted in the source programme) that, daunting as their subjects and sources might sound, they were a powerful theatrical company who knew how to 'stir and stimulate' their audience.

More than many companies, Moving Being has remained faithful to its early ideas, and in 1986 put on a highly ambitious show called *The Mabinogi*. This was a dramatisation of old Celtic folk stories, performed in the grounds of Cardiff Castle, with music by Robin Williamson (ex-Incredible String Band). It was a massive production which included a fairground, live animals, and a huge cast. Among them were local children and singers, as well as dancers Jessica Cohen and Lucy Fawcett who have gone on to perform as solo artists in their own choreography.

One of the most important trends which Moving Being established was its use of different media in performance. While the

17

company has not been the only group to do work of this kind in Britain, it has certainly helped to win acceptance for performances that cannot clearly be labelled as dance, drama, music or spectacle.

Strider

Moving Being was not exactly a dance group, and the first independent company to deal with modern, or rather post-modern dance, was Strider. This was set up by Richard Alston for just the same reason that Moore started his own group or Teresa Early started Balletmakers – to give himself the freedom to develop his own work.

Alston's approach was much more formal than the dramatic Graham-based style of London Contemporary Dance Theatre. His works didn't have plots, and the choreography tended to be spare and rather cool, using clear undecorated shapes and simple actions. The movement was influenced by a combination of Cunningham technique, ballet and T'ai Chi, and Alston frequently explored ways in which dance could relate to sound and to visual images.

Headlong (1973) was a piece about falling and flying, with movement based on runs, balances and falls. The dancers wore khaki flying-suits, and the piece was accompanied by a tape made by Anna Lockwood. This last was a mixture of a soundtrack from a Tom and Jerry cartoon, Lockwood's husband Harvey Matusow telling funny stories, and a tape of US airmen counting down to lift-off. It was a jumble of sounds that did not try to explain the choreography, but provided an 'environment' of sound for it.

Alston was also interested in taking dance to unusual venues like gyms, church halls, galleries and outdoor spaces; Strider occasionally performed in institutions too, like the memorable time it appeared at HM Prison Wormwood Scrubs. Alston described the event in an interview for *Time Out* (13 July 1973):

Wormwood Scrubs was a different experience to put it mildly. The prisoners were expecting go go dancers and as we were performing for the long-term wing (the murderers and so on) the warden said he'd give us a medal if we survived. How we eventually avoided trouble was to spread the word that it was

STRIDER

NEW DANCES AT THE PLACE, 17 DUKES ROAD, W.C.1.   SATURDAY 21st JULY 8PM.
TICKETS 44p(VAT inc.) AVAILABLE PERFORMANCE DAY ONLY.

Strider is returning to the Place for the first time since they began
in August last year. They are bringing a programme of dances all of
which are new to London.
WINGS by Sally Potter, is for a trio of girls in white and a suspended
man, this is its first public performance.
NEEDLESS ALLEY is a cooperative piece, with moving lights and trailing
sand by Charles Paton.
HEADLONG by Richard Alston is about flying and falling from great
heights, with a Gulbenkian commissioned tape score by Anna Lockwood,
it is for the four dancers of the company, in flying suits.
There are also three untitled works which will have their first public
performance, by Diana Davies, Richard Alston and Russell Dumas/
Jacqueline Lansley/Charles Paton(in collaboration).

Richard Alston's new piece is to live music by the Majorca Orchestra,
all of whose members play with the Portsmouth Sinfonia or used to play
with the Ross and Cromarty Orchestra. These groups attempt to make
popular, music not dependant on technical ability and professional
ease. They also worked with Strider at the ICA last October.

STRIDER: Richard Alsron's talented group of contemporary dancers, most
of whom trained at the Place, but are looking for a new direction-and
in many works finding it. -TIME OUT.

Programme for an early Strider performance, 1972.

a cultural event, so none of the toughies came . . . The prisoners shouted comments all the way through, often quite
funny remarks. They liked the Everly Brothers pieces the best
[by Jacky Lansley] and were really pleased we came I think.

Alston's choreography did not completely dominate Strider's

repertoire, however, and other company members made their own work, often in a very different style. Some of these works incorporated other art forms or non-dance activities, like the piece called *Hundreds and Thousands* (1972) made by Diana Davies, Jacky Lansley and Sally Potter, shown at the ICA. From Fergus Early's description, it sounds closer to performance art than dance:

> The audience is banked on two sides of the action, confronting each other over the heads of the performers. To the incompetent strains of the Ross & Cromarty Orchestra (child of the Portsmouth Sinfonia), the famous or rather infamous amateur orchestra . . . three women, clad in white tunics swing white indian clubs in unison callisthenics. To one side, the sculptor Barry Flanagan and another, perhaps Dennis Greenwood, shovel a large pile of gravel from one spot to another. This action continues throughout the piece. The musically illiterate orchestra turns [from a waltz] to the Dance of the Sugar Plum Fairy . . . the three women, in my memory, break into a repetitive pattern of catching, falling, dragging. The shovelling goes on and on.
>
> (Paper for Chisenhale/NODM weekend, May 1986, p. 2)

In 1974 Alston and other members of Strider became interested in the work of Mary Fulkerson. They spent some time at Dartington, choreographing and improvising work with her and learning about release and contact improvisation (see Dartington pp. 23–25; Glossary). At this time Alston began making what he describes as 'low energy contemplative works, with a little bit of contact in them'. And even more than before he concentrated on exploring the basic principles of dance: the use of the body's weight, the kinds of shapes it could form, and simple gestures and actions like rolling, sitting, walking and touching. The dancers wore plain baggy practice clothes to allow for unrestricted movement and to prevent the eye from being distracted. Some works were improvised during performance and some were made specially for the different venues they appeared in. Alston's interest in juxtaposing visual images with movement was highlighted in the piece he made which appeared in the same gallery as an exhibition of drawings by Jasper Johns (see Glossary). At the beginning Strider had received enthusiastic

Strider at the Serpentine Gallery, Kensington Gardens, with an exhibition of drawings by Jasper Johns.

comments from the press and the public, particularly in response to Alston's own work, which certain critics regarded as classical in its purity and clarity of movement. The company was also given several project grants (see Glossary) by the Arts Council. However, Alston's later work was less well received, and he remembers the Arts Council advising him to stop wasting his grant, to get up off the floor and do some 'real' dancing. The resistance of funding bodies to innovative work, and their unwillingness to finance it, was to become a major issue in the New Dance movement. However Alston had no intention of staying with Strider for ever, particularly if the Arts Council was going to try and dictate to him. He agreed not to apply for another grant and in 1976 he left for America to study with Cunningham.

During its three years, Strider's membership changed several times – at various points it included Diana Davies, Dennis Greenwood, Sally Potter, Eva Karczag, Jacky Lansley, Christopher Banner, Wendy Levett, Maedée Duprès, Nanette Hassall and Russell Dumas. At certain points it was run on very co-operative lines, at others Alston was more obviously in the

21

position of director. However it was still much more democrati-
cally run than traditional dance companies, since the dancers
were free to make their own work, many decisions were taken
jointly, and there was no kind of hierarchical differentiation
between the members.

Limited Dance Company

This two-woman group was formed in 1974 by Jacky Lansley
and Sally Potter as a way of developing their own special interests. Both choreographers wanted to confront political issues in
their work, and in particular to challenge the kind of female
stereotypes that prevailed in dance and the outside world (the
fragile ballerina for instance, or the *femme fatale*). They were also
trying to expand the whole concept of the dance performance
by including other art forms and everyday activities.

During their time with Strider, both Lansley and Potter had
started working on these ideas. They had made pieces that
examined the role of women, and they had combined dance
with the manipulation of bizarre props and with pedestrian
actions (see *Hundreds and Thousands*, p. 20).

But the work they made for Limited Dance Company took
these ideas even further. In their efforts to explore 'a new female
imagery' they dressed up in startling costumes; they used songs,
words, mime and props, and they incorporated other forms like
cabaret, music hall and performance art into their work. They
not only appeared in art galleries but in public places that were
not normally associated with dance. One performance they gave,
for example, was at Oxford's Museum of Modern Art where an
exhibition of Frank Stella's paintings was being held. Lansley and
Potter performed in the same gallery as the exhibition, and their
work was, as Lansley says 'a kind of dialogue with it'. They were
trying to draw the audience's attention to the fact that they were
two women performing the traditionally female art of dance, in
a space that was normally reserved for the male-dominated
world of painting, and to raise questions about why these distinctions continued to exist.

A device which they frequently used to challenge stereotyped
attitudes towards women was to wear extremely glamorous
costumes in the context of strange and disturbing situations.
Lansley described one of their performances at Lochilpaed in

Scotland, which was part of the Edinburgh Arts '74 Programme:

> Two women emerged from the sea in black evening dresses, with flippers on their feet, into a moving tableau which had been previously set up around the swings, paddling pool and public benches on the sea front; and they were met in the pool by two corresponding white figures who had moved down the main street, gathering litter.
>
> (J. Lansley: 'The Centre Line',
> paper for Chisenhale/NODM weekend, May 1986, p. 2)

Often the point was made very simply by the use of almost surrealist props, like the piece where the two of them, dressed in high heels and fur coats, carried enormous planks of wood instead of handbags.

Limited Dance Company was initially given money by The Place and received an Arts Council bursary for the following year. Between 1974 and 1975 Lansley and Potter had very successful tours in Britain, America and Europe, teaching and performing in various art institutions. And Lansley thinks that one reason why they were given so much support was that they were regarded as performance artists, rather than as dancers. Performance art was treated as a branch of the visual arts, which at that time had more funding and a higher status than dance. There was also a much larger and more sophisticated audience for this kind of work among visual artists, since, as Lansley says, 'the dance world then was still very conservative in its tastes'.

By 1975 however, Lansley had begun to feel that Limited Dance Company was taking her away from her roots, so it was disbanded and she went back to more dance-oriented work. But her choreography continued to incorporate mime, words, props, music, song and striking visual images, and in this respect her work has certain links with that of choreographers like Ian Spink, Fergus Early and Laurie Booth.

Dartington

While much of this new experimental choreography came out of The Place, another important centre of activity was Dartington College of Arts in Devon. During the 1940s and 1950s this college had been closely associated with European modern dance –

both Rudolf Laban and Kurt Jooss made their base there. By 1963 it had established a course for teachers of modern dance which was heavily based on the Graham technique. Then in 1973 the whole style and structure of the course was drastically revised by the new head of dance, Mary Fulkerson.

Mary Fulkerson had been invited over from America, where she had been in close contact with the post-modern dance scene. During the late 1960s and early 1970s she had developed her own very radical approach to teaching, which had evolved out of dissatisfactions with her own training.

As a student she had disliked the competitive atmosphere of her course, and the fact that she was expected to work towards a standard level of perfection rather than being taught to value her own skills and qualities. She had also felt that too many dance classes were taught by a system of repetition and imitation, so that students could not explore in detail how the body functioned – how the muscles and joints worked, how the weight should be placed and how a movement was affected by tension or relaxation. Above all, she had been frustrated by the fact that only certain kinds of movement were accepted as dance – anything else being dismissed as graceless or unskilled.

Reacting against this limited perception, Fulkerson had begun making dances that used not only non-dance movement, but also non-dancers. She had been curious to see how movement looked on 'ordinary bodies' – and though she was regarded as a rebel in her own college, she started to meet others who thought along similar lines and helped her to develop her ideas.

The first important influence was Jean Skinner who taught her the basic principles of release (see Glossary); the second was Steve Paxton, one of the early pioneers of contact improvisation (see Glossary). Through these people Fulkerson developed her interest in improvised and non-technique-based movement, and evolved the teaching methods that she brought to Dartington. In her classes, students were encouraged to discover their own style of moving, strict technique was rarely taught, and the atmosphere was always relaxed and exploratory. Steve Paxton himself came over at regular intervals to teach at the college.

Many of the choreographers closely associated with New Dance were trained by, or had some connection with Fulkerson (including Rosemary Butcher, Sue MacLennan, Richard Alston and Yolande Snaith). Her influence on the development of New

Dance was crucial not only because she introduced release and contact improvisation to this country (two of the styles most often associated with New Dance) but also because she demonstrated alternative ways of teaching dance – ways that were not oppressively competitive and did not demand a rigid degree of perfection.

Fulkerson's own work has also influenced other choreographers like Ian Spink. It often incorporates props, costumes and sections of spoken narrative which convey the thoughts, feelings and fantasies of a particular character. Each work for Fulkerson is an exploration of how movements and ideas can spark each other off by a process of association.

In 1987 Katie Duck took Fulkerson's place as head of dance, and by this time Dartington was firmly established as a major centre for New Dance. Its students were trained in the experimental, alternative atmosphere that had characterised the early days at The Place; visiting teachers brought new ideas from abroad and above all, the annual Dartington festival provided a showcase for new choreography.

The birth of New Dance

The setting up of The Place and the changes at Dartington College were all crucial to the beginning of the New Dance movement. Yet it was not until the formation of the group X6 and the magazine *New Dance* that dancers and choreographers started to think of themselves in terms of a larger group, rather than as isolated individuals exploring their own ideas.

X6 – an alternative space for dance

The main motive for starting up the X6 collective was to give practical help to those dancers and choreographers who were no longer in the protective environment of institutions like The Place. Finding space that was cheap enough, warm enough and large enough to rehearse in, finding teachers with whom to take class, and having a place in which to share and discover new ideas were continual problems for many independent artists. And if a new work was to be performed, the additional problems of finding the dancers, of booking a suitable venue, and of getting

25

out advance publicity were even more difficult to solve. Teresa Early had faced some of these issues in Balletmakers Ltd and in 1976 another group of dancers, calling themselves X6, tried to find new solutions to them.

The first step towards forming the collective was taken in 1975. A small group of dancers including Fergus Early, Maedée Duprès, Jacky Lansley and Emilyn Claid had collaborated on a performance for the International Contemporary Music Festival in Royan, France. On their return, Duprès, Claid and Early decided to continue working together. Together with Craig Givens and Timothy Lamford they made another piece for the Serpentine Gallery, and tried to find a settled base from which to operate.

Their first home was at The International Arts Centre at the Elephant and Castle, London, but it lacked heating and was poorly administered, so they moved to an old marble factory in the nearby Walworth Road. Here they were joined by Jacky Lansley and Mary Prestidge (a former Olympic gymnast and one-time dancer with Ballet Rambert) and they started to run classes and hold discussions. The venue turned out to be just as unsatisfactory as the Arts Centre studio however, and they knew that they could not get any kind of effective organisation under way until they had found the right space in which to work.

After much searching, the group discovered a spacious well-lit room with a wooden floor in some disused dockland buildings at Butler's Wharf. By April 1976 they had moved into what became known as the X6 dance space, and the collective organisation of dancers known by the same name was unofficially launched.

The opening was celebrated with a short Sunday performance devised by Lansley. It was one of the first in a series of works by her and Early which reworked ballet classics from a modern perspective. Early recalls that it was set to the music from Act II of *Swan Lake* with 'Mary Prestidge as a sort of gymnastic flying swan, Jacky and Emilyn as big fast moving swans, Maedée and myself in the Odette/Siegfried duet: all of us in baggy beige tropical suits' (Paper for Chisenhale/NODM weekend, May 1986, p. 4).

The performance was followed by a meeting of the collective (now comprising Mary Prestidge, Jacky Lansley, Emilyn Claid, Fergus Early and Maedée Duprès), in which they began to plan their future activities. These included a major performance event *By River and Wharf* (described below); a three-week summer school to be called a 'Radical Dance Summer School'; a conference on experimental dance (the first to be held in England); and a new magazine to be called *New Dance*.

By River and Wharf was an afternoon-long performance which took place around Bermondsey docklands in June 1976. As the audience strolled around the area, they encountered a series of dance performances which had all been devised for their special location – 'across Tower Bridge, down alleys, on old bomb-sites, suspended from Victorian girders, deep in Thames mud, on the grass of an urban square, beneath high rise flats' (Early's paper for Chisenhale/NODM weekend, May 1986, p. 4). It was an event that resembled the scale of Meredith Monk's work at The Place in 1972 (see p. 8) and many of the people involved in it were to be closely associated with the New Dance movement for the next decade. These were not just the members of the collective but also Rosemary Butcher, Craig Givens, Dennis Greenwood, Julyen Hamilton and Eva Karczag. The work was also characteristic of the interests that many New Dance choreographers were to pursue – it was made collaboratively rather than by a single individual; it explored ways in which dance could be presented outside traditional theatres, and above all it presented dance to a community audience.

For the X6 collective and those connected with them, having their own space was like a guarantee of freedom. It was a place in which they could meet, in which they could administer all their activities, and it allowed them not only to choose exactly what kind of classes and workshops they wanted, but also to run them in the way they believed was right. Even more than Balletmakers, which had had no such permanent base, it provided a genuine alternative to the established dance institutions.

The classes and workshops held at X6 were open to anyone who wanted to attend and, as time went on, they covered a wide range of different movement techniques. These included T'ai Chi, Cunningham, release work, contact improvisation, gymnastics, and a basic form of ballet that was stripped of its conventional decorative style. All classes were taught in a relaxed, non-competitive atmosphere and dancers were encouraged to develop their own personal style of movement rather than to strive for some 'objective' standard. Composition classes were also run, with Lansley continuing her interest in combining theatrical elements with dance. One course of classes was, significantly, run for women only.

At first most of the classes were taught by members of the collective, but by the end of 1976 contact had been made with Dartington. Mary Fulkerson started to give workshops at X6, introducing the members to release and image work, and she encouraged people like Steve Paxton and Lisa Nelson (another American dancer) to teach contact classes there. This close connection between X6 and Dartington was very important, since it allowed students graduating from the college to continue the kind of training they had received there. It also gave them space to make and perform work. Certain students from The Place and the Laban Centre also began to use X6, and continued to do so when the whole set-up moved to its new home in Chisenhale Road, East London, in 1981.

The politics of New Dance

Feminism

X6 did not just provide an alternative space for dance, it also allowed people to discuss new ways of thinking about the art form. The idea that dance was simply a high-class brand of entertainment was something which the collective questioned right from the beginning. They believed that dance should be aware of live political and social issues – and one of the most important questions which they debated was feminism and the treatment of women in dance.

The collective was unanimous in arguing that women are very constricted in dance, particularly in ballet. Most ballerinas (they felt) are expected to conform to a very particular physical type with long, slender limbs, a small head and a pretty face. However demanding her role, she is expected to appear delicate and light – lifted and displayed by her male partner but never supporting him in return. And the kinds of women that she portrays are very limited. Most female roles in ballet portray idealised heroines or evil villainesses; they rarely show women as complex and distinctive individuals.

Rejecting these received ideas, Lansley and the others argued that there are fine women dancers who are tall, broad and muscular, just as there are fine men who are short and slender, and

NEW DANCE

Quarterly 50p   No 5 New Year '78

Cover of *New Dance* magazine (No. 5, New Year 1978).

that there is no justification for their exclusion from professional companies. They also looked to contact improvisation as proof that women could lift men if they were properly taught and could participate equally in partnering.

These ideas were given more tangible form in some of the works they made, which were often reinterpretations of classical ballets. By challenging the traditional image of the ballerina, the collective hoped to challenge the way in which women are treated in society, the ways in which they are punished if they are 'ugly', if they demand their own power, if they refuse to be obedient, if they want to choose their own life-style or career.

Bleeding Fairies, made by Claid, Prestidge and Lansley in 1977 made the point that ballerinas are real, flesh and blood (and menstruating) women, not ethereal and romantic beings. The piece used dance, song and 'play' to explore some of the most basic female images in Western culture – 'the witch, the whore, the fairy, Mother Earth, images which reflect society's moral/religious distinctions between good and bad women'. It was, Lansley recalls, a 'chaotic, aggressive' kind of performance, in which the dancers disrupted the ordinary ways in which women were meant to perform:

> At one point we formed a series of classical tableaux made up of balletic poses . . . Gradually our pace quickened and our poses became more and more macho and 'attacking' until eventually we had destroyed the classical tableau structure, breaking out in a display of aggressive virtuosity.
>
> (*New Dance* No. 6, Spring 1978, p. 11)

Lansley's *I, Giselle* (1981) retold the story of Giselle, showing her not as a victim but as a powerful woman who becomes triumphant through death. It was a piece involving speech and songs as well as dance and it had music composed by Steve Montague. Much of the movement was based on ballet and most of the story followed the original scenario. Lansley knew the original ballet well and admired it: 'It wasn't a flippant use of the material at all, we felt the ballet was very strong, both structurally and choreographically. We wanted to keep the strengths of the original but subvert its ideology' (interview with author, 1985).

There were five performers in the ballet. Early was Albrecht (the Prince who betrays Giselle in the original story); Chris Cheek was Hilarion (the peasant who loves her) and there were two Giselles – Suzy Gilmour for Act I, which contained a lot of dialogue, and Sue MacLennan for Act II, in which there was much more dancing. Lansley herself doubled as Berthe (Giselle's mother) and the Queen of the Wilis. These parts were treated as two aspects of the same powerful woman, a woman who can wield strong magic and who advises Giselle to leave Albrecht. In this version Giselle sees through Albrecht and is not duped by him at all. When she 'dies' and becomes a Wili, it is not a tragic event, but a choice to enter a more powerful and exclusively female territory.

There were other innovations in the interpretation too, like the 'mad scene', where everyone goes crazy on stage, and Chris Cheek becomes a tyrannical ballet-master who whips the dancers on to greater efforts. Over all it was a highly polished and entertaining piece, accessible in ways that did not compromise its political message – and it played to packed audiences at the Drill Hall in London for three weeks.

Other political themes

Although feminism was the most recurrent theme in works made by the collective, other political questions were not ignored. During a conference that was held at the first ADMA festival (May/June 1977), Jacky Lansley argued that if dancers could make people conscious of social and political issues through their work, then they could help to change society. Examples of work that tried to do this are Julyen Hamilton and Timothy Lamford's duet at the 1977 ADMA festival (see p. 65) which questioned male stereotypes and the glamour of violence, and Laurie Booth's *Animal Parts* (1984) (see p. 84) which looked at how we treat animals.

Emilyn Claid believed that even if choreographers did not choose to make work with political content, they should always be conscious of the politics of their situation. For her, the most important principle of New Dance was that people should make connections between themselves, their work and the outside world:

> There is no one way of working or type of dance that can be labelled New Dance. New Dance is about making connections to the environment, to the social context, to the city, to the financial context, to the world . . . Each individual, whether learning, performing, teaching, criticising, dancing, writing about dance or supporting dance can have a unique method of making the connections.
>
> (*New Dance* No. 3, 1977, p. 2)

31

Not everyone associated with the New Dance movement agreed with this political stance however. Rosemary Butcher, for instance, said at the same ADMA conference that she no longer wanted 'to analyse or justify her work, she was simply concerned with dance as a pure abstract art form' (*New Dance* No. 3, 1977, p. 16).

Collective organisation

Politics was not just an important subject for choreography, it also entered into the way in which the organisation was run. Like many other alternative organisations at that time (feminist groups, certain theatre companies, radical political groups etc.) the group believed in the importance of complete democracy. X6 was therefore run as a collective, with everyone making important decisions together, as well as sharing all the menial tasks like cleaning and putting up posters. This was very different from traditional dance institutions which are usually run by a few powerful individuals.

Collective principles also extended to some of the works made by members of X6, namely those in which several people developed the ideas and the movement rather than one person telling the other dancers what to do. Some of the problems associated with this kind of work were debated at a conference at X6 in the summer of 1976. Most people agreed that it allowed everyone to work creatively – that the dancers were more than tools in someone else's vision. But some argued that the collective process was not likely to produce strong work. It would be better for one person to make the final artistic decisions, even if others might contribute to the piece through improvisation or discussion.

Critics, criticism and a new critical language

Knowing how indifferent the press had been to Balletmakers, members of the New Dance movement made every effort to get their work seen by the critics, and understood by them. They knew that if they wanted to attract new audiences to dance, particularly experimental dance, and if they wanted to get funding for it, they would need some kind of publicity and discussion in newspapers and magazines.

Critics' reviews obviously have a strong influence on the box office, but press coverage is important in other ways too.

Previews and features provide crucial publicity for events, and a positive article can give helpful background information about a particular work. Press articles may also influence funding bodies when they assess grants for a company or an artist.

During the 1970s and for much of the 1980s it proved very difficult to get national coverage of small, independent dance events. At first a number of critics were unwilling to go to performances – partly because they were so different from ballet and mainstream modern dance, and partly because they tended to take place in uncomfortable, out-of-the-way venues. Even more frustratingly, most of those who did attend had little idea about what they were seeing and often applied irrelevant critical standards to it. They complained that dancers were not pointing their feet or did not have high extensions, even when the style of the choreography was meant to be relaxed; they criticised the lack of action in a piece even if the choreographer was exploring slow movement and stillness; and they became irritated with the absence of a clear theme even if the point of the work was its use of different images or narrative fragments.

Discussing the first ADMA festival of new dance work (1977) Emilyn Claid complained that few critics seemed interested by the opportunity to see a broad cross-section of new choreography. She felt that they were doing nothing to help either themselves or the public to understand experimental dance. 'If people's image of the long-legged flying ballerina is their idea of excellence then there is nothing that the national critics are going to do to change it' (*New Dance* No. 3, 1977, p. 7).

The indifference, and even hostility towards much new choreography was not just an initial reaction – it was still current in the 1980s. Chris Crickmay in 'The Apparently Invisible Dances of Miranda Tufnell and Dennis Greenwood' (*New Dance* No. 21, pp. 7–8) contrasted a review in *The Sunday Times* of a performance by Tufnell and Greenwood and comments by Steve Paxton on the same event. The former called it an 'evening of British rubbish' by people who had 'never grown up'; the latter used terms like 'humorous, intelligent, mysterious and elegant.' The point, as Crickmay argued, is not that newspaper critic didn't like what he saw – all artists expect some adverse criticism – but that his dismissive account of it made no effort to understand what is happening. He cited the following passage as an example:

33

In *Night Pieces* a man in an overcoat intoned an interminable monologue of gobbledegook while sitting on and falling off a chair, and two dancers pawed the ground, pausing to switch hanging lights on and off. It was during *Other Rooms*, at the point where Miss Tufnell was crawling on all fours with a table on her back and a lamp dangling from her teeth, that I realised these people have never grown up.

Crickmay's argument is that anyone reading this review is likely to be put off the performance, and that given the size of the paper's circulation, a lot of readers would be likely to develop ill-informed prejudice against similarly experimental choreography.

While the collective spent some time and effort trying to persuade the press to attend new dance performances they were also convinced that the independent dance scene should be developing its own critics and its own voice. So in 1977 they produced the first issue of the quarterly magazine *New Dance*, which, like X6, was run collectively, with everyone involved in both its writing and its production.

Initially the members of the *New Dance* collective were almost the same as the X6 membership, but other people rapidly became involved and there was always an open invitation for readers to contribute their own letters, articles and reviews. As the magazine increased in circulation, alternative ideas about dance began to reach a much wider public; dancers and choreographers had a new forum for sharing information and opinions, and above all the magazine was one of the few outlets for detailed and sympathetic accounts of experimental choreography.

The writers of *New Dance* were not only committed to describing innovative work, they also played with different approaches to reviewing. Some offered a straightforward, descriptive record of the movement, some were very personal in their response, some works were reviewed by their own creators and some were discussed in terms of their social and political implications. At times the magazine was accused of incestuousness, of being concerned only with a small group of choreographers and ignoring wider areas of dance (see letter from Geoff Moore, *New Dance* No. 7, 1978 p. 10). There have also been times when the standard of writing and production have been less that professional. But whatever its weaknesses, the magazine is one of the few available records of experimental dance during the 1970s and early 1980s, and it has always been an energetic forum for debate. Its closure in 1988 has left a significant gap in the New Dance scene.

Funding

In his paper for the Chisenhale/NODM weekend Fergus Early writes, 'Funding was and is the key issue. New Dance opposes oppression and oppression is always economically based' (p. 1).

Though X6 and *New Dance* provided space and an independent voice for artists, they were still faced with the problem of finding money to make new work. With little or no funding, choreographers could only work on isolated projects, often having to do other jobs to scrape a living. They were limited in the number of dancers they could afford and in the size of space they could rent, and they could rarely consider using original design or music. All of these constrictions made it difficult for them to develop their ideas fully.

The magazine, the collective and ADMA (see below) did everything they could to draw attention to the inadequate way in which independent dance was funded. What they objected to in particular were the following:

(1) Dance had no separate panel to speak for it at the Arts Council (until 1980 dance was part of the Music Panel).

(2) There were few sympathetic and informed people dealing with the application for funds for experimental dance works.

(3) Very little of the total dance budget went to independent work. (In the first issue of *New Dance* (Spring 1977, p. 21), Fergus Early claimed that only 0.5% of the total budget for dance went to independent choreographers. And though John Cruft, Music Director of the Arts Council argued that the figure was actually around 3%, the sum was still very low.)

(4) All the money for independent dance came in the form of project funding rather than revenue funding (see Glossary).

(5) There was little financial support for dance outside London, and little attempt to develop it.

In the Autumn of 1976 a group called the Association of Dance and Mime Artists (ADMA) was formed, with the help of certain people from X6. It was a much larger organisation than the one at Butler's Wharf, with a membership from all over the country, and with a steering committee based in London. Through this committee (which was meant to represent a national voice) ADMA hoped to meet with the Arts Council on a regular basis and to press for reform. Like X6, the organisation was run on collective principles and believed passionately in the importance of dancers organising themselves to assert their own power.

The organisation's aims were very similar to those of X6 – namely to get proper representation of experimental dance on the grant-funding bodies and to educate audiences and critics in the new kinds of choreography that were emerging. Only when new forms of dance were properly understood could they be judged fairly and funded adequately.

ADMA also believed that new ideas as well as new work should be funded: that choreographers experimenting in innovative areas should be given grants even if the work they produced was not up to 'professional standards'. Such new work was risky and might not always be successful, but it was important that the risks could be taken if dance was to develop as an art form.

From the outset ADMA was faced with one serious obstacle: funding for the arts was no longer as generous as it had been during the late 1960s and early 1970s. New dance was competing with experimental work in other art forms for a share in a shrinking budget.

Yet despite this, ADMA was instrumental in winning some of the battles that determined the course of independent British dance. For example, in 1977:

(1) There was an increase in money available for project grants and therefore new work.

(2) The Greater London Arts Association (GLAA) appointed its first dance officer – Val Bourne – who was also the first regional dance officer in the country. Though GLAA only gave a small amount of money to dance, Bourne was committed to funding experimental projects. Even more important, she set up a small-scale touring circuit in the outer

London boroughs – using schools, church halls and community centres. This had three important results: first, it opened up new venues for performers – it was always a problem finding space to perform; second, it developed a wider audience for new dance; and third, because many of the groups were encouraged to give workshops, more people became interested in doing as well as in watching dance.

(3) Dance became more strongly established outside London. East Midlands Arts set up its own dance company called EMMA. And in December North-West Arts started to give revenue funding to Ludus, a dance-in-education company based in Lancaster.

And in 1978:

(1) Seven groups were offered funding for a year, including X6 – though there were warnings that this might involve cuts in money available to project grants.

(2) GLAA offered five dance fellowships to pay for individual dancers to work inside the community, organising classes, workshops and performances.

(3) Dance continued to grow outside London. In addition to Ludus and EMMA there was East Anglian Dance Theatre and Merseyside Dance. Jumpers, a company based in Wales, had actually had their grant cut, but they continued work, and the Cardiff-based Moving Being was also still being funded.

By the end of 1980, the Arts Council had awarded dance its own separate department, under the direction of Jane Nicholas. Dance was finally recognised as an art form in its own right, on an equal basis with music, drama, literature and the visual arts.

Expansion phase 1: 1976–80

As a result of new developments in the dance world – the founding of The Place, X6 and *New Dance* magazine, the growth of open classes and workshops – increasing numbers of dancers and choreographers made contact with each other and the number of small independent dance companies grew dramatically (see Appendix).

These companies set the pattern for the development of new and experimental dance. Most of them were very small (choreographers could rarely afford to pay their dancers) and most of them worked on a shoestring budget. Some of the luckier groups received project grants, but as these were only offered for the creation of individual works, many companies only came together at certain times, with the dancers rehearsing and performing the project and then disbanding, either to join another group, or to earn money doing something completely different. (If you read through programmes or cast lists, you see the same names continually cropping up in different companies.)

Restrictions like these meant that most new choreography featured few dancers and only a basic level of music and design. Some choreographers created this kind of work by choice – because they disliked the large scale, elaborate productions of ballet and mainstream modern dance companies – but others were genuinely frustrated by the fact they could not work continuously with the same group of dancers and develop more ambitious ideas.

At first the growth of new companies was limited by the lack of venues and rehearsal space – X6 and the artist-run Action Space at the Drill Hall, became very much in demand. But slowly, more venues started to show an interest in dance, and audiences for new dance began to grow.

By the late 1970s, London dance venues included The Place Theatre, Riverside Studios, the ICA, Oval House, Battersea Arts Centre, Jackson's Lane Community Centre, The Roundhouse and the ACME Gallery. Outside London, small theatres, colleges, arts centres and art galleries began to open their doors to dance. The Arnolfini Gallery in Bristol is a good example of how venues began to programme dance into their activities. In 1976 it organised a whole dance season, which included Another Dance Group, Rosemary Butcher, and Basic Space, and in the same year it presented a day of dance organised by the London School of Contemporary Dance which brought together experienced teachers from London and local amateur groups. In 1978 Janet Smith gave a weekend residency, and as Dance Umbrella (see pp. 44–46) spread its programme to include regional tours, the Arnolfini presented many of its participants.

But dance in the regions was not just a question of London companies giving occasional performances outside the capital – a number of small companies began to base themselves in different parts of the country, and to receive support from Regional Arts Associations. Generally limited to five or six dancers, these companies created work that was on a sufficiently small and flexible scale to fit any kind of venue. Whereas the larger touring companies like Rambert and London Contemporary Dance Theatre could only perform in well-equipped theatres in large towns, these smaller groups brought a range of dance (some of it experimental, some of it in a more mainstream modern style) to small towns and villages, appearing in village halls, schools and community centres. Most of them also gave workshops and classes, helping audiences to understand performances and encouraging them to dance themselves.

Several projects were also initiated to link dance more closely to the community. In 1976 Molly Kenny was appointed co-ordinator of the Cardiff Community Dance Project (funded by the Welsh Arts Council) which was a scheme to encourage more of the general public to participate in dance activities. (By 1980 the project was running courses and classes in a wide range of techniques for over four hundred students as well as an annual intensive course to give teenagers a taste of professional training.) In 1977 a similar project was started at Bristol, and in 1978 Marie McClusky (who had once trained at The Place) began teaching dance classes at Swindon. She remembers the town as 'a desert' when she first began, but within ten years her classes blossomed into a full timetable of dance activities for both children and adults, as well as a full-time foundation course for those hoping to enter serious dance training.

Other important work was done with young, mainly black dancers by Nadine Senior in Harehills School, Leeds, (on the basis of which the new Northern School of Contemporary Dance was founded), and by Veronica Lewis, who started up the Cheshire Dance Workshop with funds from the Gulbenkian Foundation. By the 1980s, local councils and Regional Arts Associations were beginning to appoint dance animateurs throughout the country, individuals whose role was to coordinate local dance companies, teachers, schools and so on.

Although much of this community dance activity involved movement forms that were not specifically associated with New Dance – like jazz, tap, disco, Graham and Cunningham techniques – it all stemmed from a conviction shared by the New Dance movement that dance is not just an exclusive art form, but an activity that should be open to everyone.

Festivals

Another way of judging the growth of independent dance is to look at the size and popularity of the dance festivals, which became an important feature of the whole independent scene. Often lasting up to five or six weeks, these events were important showcases for new works, and provided crucial practical assistance for their staging. Projects which would not fill a whole programme could be shown alongside other works. Companies which could not afford their own publicity, lighting, sound systems etc. could make use of those laid on by the festival. More generally, festivals allowed artists to share each other's ideas, and they helped to publicise what was happening in dance. Critics and audiences who might not attend a single performance might be attracted to see new works because of the publicity and excitement surrounding the 'big event'.

ADMA
One of the first major festivals was held by ADMA in May and June 1977 at the Drill Hall in Chenies Street, London. Like ADMA itself, it was very much a self-help event, set up and administered by the dancers. The festival was open to anyone, which meant that the standard of performance was very varied, ranging, as Fergus Early said, 'from the superb to the embarrassing' (paper for Chisenhale/NODM weekend, p. 4). But it also meant that choreographers had the chance to explore new ideas and even to make mistakes in front of a largely sympathetic audience.

The performances at this festival were from artists working both in London and the regions. They included works by people associated with X6, like Fergus Early and Emilyn Claid; by companies from outside London, like Janet Smith and Dancers, and Cycles; and they ranged from experimental dance to Indian dance (a Kathak [see Glossary] recital by Alpana Sengupta) and mime (Moving Picture Mime Show). Reviews and descriptions of many of these can be found in *New Dance* No. 3.

Other important events in the festival were its daily classes and workshops, as well as its opportunities for discussion. There were unofficial meetings between dancers, as well as the official Festival Seminar, all of which allowed individual dancers and choreographers to share ideas and appreciate each other's work.

Another important festival was held in July that year, the Many Ways of Moving Conference, which took place at the Polytechnic of Central London and at The Place. As its title suggests, the conference was meant to introduce people to different approaches to dance. A series of practical workshops taught the basic principles of ballet, folk, gymnastics, New Dance, martial

FESTIVAL OF DANCE AND MIME

presented by ADMA 23 May-11 June

THE ASSOCIATION OF DANCE AND MIME ARTISTS Festival is the biggest showcase in the country for new dance and movement theatre.
This year in our second festival over 60 performers and performing groups are brought together

for the festival's three weeks: you can see three, four, or more groups in a single day, as well as joining in classes, workshops and seminars with some of the most interesting artists working in dance and mime today, who come to the festival from all over Britain and from abroad.

Programme for the second ADMA festival (1978).

arts, classical Indian dance, yoga and so on, and there were discussions on how dance could be used in medicine, and its function in education and recreation, as well as its development as a theatrical art.

ADMA held its second festival in 1978; in some ways it was more successful than the first. There were three times as many performers, more classes, and the whole event received greater attention from the press. However the increased numbers put a heavy strain on the festival's organisers – the schedule of performances was overcrowded and some events started late and could not be properly rehearsed. Inevitably too, with so many performances, the standard was even more uneven than the previous year, and the festival was accused of amateurishness.

There were notable exceptions, like *Sergeant Early's Dream* by Fergus Early, and Richard Alston's *Doublework*. But the Arts Council felt that the general standard of performances was unacceptably low, and told ADMA that it would have to drop its open-door policy and weed out the less polished work if it wanted to be given money in the future. Even those who were more sympathetic to ADMA, like Teresa Early, were critical of the over-all quality of the work. She felt that the *idea* of experimentation had been allowed to excuse too many unprofessional performances, giving as an example a piece by Sarah Green and Mary Prestidge in which the words spoken could not be heard by the audience (see *New Dance* No. 7, 1978 pp. 8–9).

ADMA defended its position by arguing that the point of the festival was to *avoid* competition in dance. It felt that everyone should have the chance to try out new ideas, and to see each other's work, even if it wasn't completely polished. The Association did not hold another festival however, and its place was taken by two other new festivals, Dartington and Dance Umbrella.

Dartington

The first Dartington festival was a small affair which took place in June 1978. American performers like Steve Paxton appeared alongside British companies like Richard Alston and Dancers, and Janet Smith and Dancers, and a few classes and workshops were held. At the time it was seen as a regional extension of the ADMA festival, but in following years it replaced the latter as Britain's most important open dance festival. Work in progress and work by relatively unknown choreographers was welcome, though most choreography that was shown tended to reflect the styles of dance associated with Dartington and the X6 collective, namely release, contact improvisation, and the more political 'performance work' of choreographers like Jacky Lansley.

As the Dartington festival grew in size, it developed into an intensive five-day programme of classes and performances. Participants camped or stayed nearby, classes started first thing in the morning and went on till late afternoon, and long programmes of dance were seen every lunch-time and evening.

Steve Paxton teaching a class at Dartington, 1980. Photo: Chris Ha.

43

There was always an intimate informal atmosphere in which new ideas were given a sympathetic reception.

In any year, audiences could see work by former Dartington students and fledgling companies, pieces by established choreographers like Rosemary Butcher and Sue MacLennan, and also new work by foreign artists, such as the Florence-based company Katie Duck and Group O. Many of the Dartington discoveries, like Katie Duck, have subsequently gone on to perform at the larger, and now more prestigious Dance Umbrella.

Dance Umbrella

The Arts Council saw the need for a dance festival as early as 1977, but did not regard ADMA's event as a suitable basis to work from. In 1978 Val Bourne was asked to form a committee that would select the participants and organise a festival for late 1978. At the same time the ICA was preparing a season of American dance, so the two events joined forces to become the first Dance Umbrella. (The festival's policy of showing British dance alongside foreign work was thus, at first, almost an accident). It was not universally welcomed though, particularly by ADMA, which was afraid it would become an official alternative to its own festival, and would divide rather than unite the dance world.

The first Dance Umbrella took place from 7–25 November 1978 at the ICA and Riverside Studios. Several soloists came over from America – Remy Charlip, Douglas Dunn, Brooke Myers and Sara Rudner – and there was a broad cross-section of new British work, including Richard Alston and Dancers, Basic Space Dance Theatre, Rosemary Butcher Dance Company, Cycles, Maedée Duprès, Fergus Early, EMMA, Extemporary Dance Company, MAAS Movers, Janet Smith and Dancers, Robert North, East Anglia Dance Theatre and Ludus. As well as performances there were seminars dealing with dance education and administration, exhibitions of Remy Charlip's drawings, Mark Lancaster's designs for Merce Cunningham, and films, videos and workshops.

Audience attendance was high and there were enthusiastic responses from both critics and public, though Dunn's performance aroused violent controversy. Claire Hayes' review in *New Dance* (No. 9, 1978 pp. 7–8) welcomed the chance to see American performers of such professionalism and strength,

Partners in improvisation – Kirstie Simpson and Julyen Hamilton. Photo: Jac Jaeger.

though X6 pointedly ran a small festival of its own at the same time, indicating that it wished to retain a separate identity.

As a showcase for new dance work, the Umbrella was much more successful than ADMA in reaching a wide audience, and

45

proved that it was necessary to have at least one festival where the organisation was on a professional footing and where most of the work was of a polished standard. Certainly, in the years that followed, Dance Umbrella grew dramatically in size and range, running for seven and a half weeks in 1985, extending into new venues like The Place, the Almeida Theatre, and Sadler's Wells Theatre, and spreading outwards into towns like Bristol, Cardiff, Nottingham, Portsmouth and Glasgow.

As well as heightening the profile of independent dance in this country, the festival also presented important new work from abroad. Some of it was by established artists like Trisha Brown, Meredith Monk and David Gordon, some by then relatively unknown choreographers like Anne Teresa De Keersmaeker (1982), Daniel Larrieu (1983) and Compagnie Cré-Ange (1986), who have since gone on to make important names for themselves. This policy has made the dance public much more aware of what is going on outside Britain and has exposed British choreographers to a much wider range of influences.

Though Dance Umbrella started out as a dance festival, it later incorporated a management service for independent soloists and companies. During the organisation of the first festival, the committee was shocked by the inadequacy of publicity and administration for small companies. So, with funding from the Gulbenkian Foundation, it launched a trial scheme by which it could administrate several companies at the same time.

This again worried ADMA, which felt that by helping only a few privileged artists the scheme would be divisive. However other small management services have followed the Umbrella, and have developed close links with larger movements like ADMA itself and the National Organisation of Dance and Mime (NODM) (now called Dance UK).

Expansion phase 2: the 1980s

The move to Chisenhale

In 1980 the whole of Butler's Wharf was cleared for redevelopment and the X6 collective had to look for new premises. What they found was an old warehouse in Chisenhale Road, East

London, which was being converted into a series of artists' studios. The collective took over a large top-floor room, and enough space to seat a small audience.

The new Chisenhale collective, as it came to be known, included not only previous X6 members like Fergus Early, Jacky Lansley and Mary Prestidge, but also younger members like Yolande Snaith. In recent years the new venue has continued to be an important base for independent dancers, providing rehearsal and performance space, as well as a venue for meetings. But it has also created much stronger links with the local community than X6 attempted to do, running classes for children and adults in a range of dance forms – from tap to modern to contact improvisation. In its informal 'Cha Cha Cha' evenings, Chisenhale also gives important space and time to inexperienced choreographers.

Funding

Chisenhale received GLAA and Arts Council funding to help improve its amenities, but after the late 1970s the general level of dance funding declined to the point where it did not even keep pace with inflation. The abolition of the GLC (Greater London Council) in 1986 was another set-back, since it had provided much of the funding for London companies and venues.

Things did not improve during the late 1980s when dance, like all the other arts, was asked to look for money from private sources. This was particularly difficult for independent dance, which is generally seen as less prestigious than other art forms and is less attractive to sponsors than mainstream dance, opera, music and drama.

As the climate worsened during the early 1980s it became clear that something had to be done to defend the position of independent dance. It was felt that ADMA was not promoting the cause efficiently enough – its membership was dwindling and people argued that its commitment to independent artists, rather than to the whole spectrum of dance and mime, was too limited. Dance needed a strong unanimous voice to argue its case, because so many of its problems were common to every area of the art.

The first step towards the formation of the National Organisation of Dance and Mime (NODM) was taken at a meeting at the second Dance Umbrella in 1980. Dance and mime people from all over Britain attended a discussion at Riverside Studios, in order to debate the problems which dance was facing.

As a result of the meeting a working party called the Dance and Mime Action Group (DAMAG) was formed to identify the issues more clearly, and its conclusions were published in a letter in 1982. Its membership, representing a much wider spread of dance interests than that of ADMA, included Val Bourne (Dance Umbrella), John Drummond (Arts Council), Robin Howard (The Place), Norman Morrice (The Royal Ballet) and Jan Murray and Peter Williams (dance critics). But it is interesting – and depressing – to see that many of the problems they were dealing with were exactly the same as those which X6 and ADMA had identified. These included:

(1) *Space for dance.* The group argued that there should be: (a) a dance house in central London to accommodate the major British companies; and (b) studio space in central London, offering class, rehearsal and performance facilities to dance teachers, small companies and independent dance and mime artists. (X6 had fought for (b) from the beginning, but despite important steps such as the founding of Chisenhale, its aims had not nearly been realised.)

(2) *Training grants.* Pressure should be brought to bear on the Department of Education and Science to have the discretionary grants for vocational training designated as mandatory (i.e. students who are given places on official dance courses should be given at least the money for tuition fees).

(3) *Media coverage.* There should be greater coverage of dance and mime events in the press and on television (this was something that X6 and ADMA had also fought for, although members of DAMAG argued that ballet was only marginally better covered than new dance and that the media was much more interested in plays and music than in any form of dance).

(4) *Subsidy.* A campaign was needed to get greater funding for dance. The committee felt that the rapid growth in all kinds

of dance during the 1970s and 1980s justified much more money being allocated to it. Dance was still grossly under-funded in relation to the other arts. (Funding was obviously an issue that had been fought by X6 and ADMA, but they had been mostly concerned with the lack of finances for independent dance. DAMAG however argued that all dance forms were being under-funded, not just independent dance.)

After the publication of this letter the National Lobby of Dance and Mime was formed, which later changed its name to the National Organisation of Dance and Mime. As well as deal-ing with issues like funding (lobbying the Arts Council, liaising with sponsors), the organisation aimed to offer more practical help to dancers and choreographers. It investigated issues like the pension rights of salaried dancers and the possibilities of special medical insurance for dancers. It also compiled lists of rehearsal spaces available in London and of doctors with a specialist knowledge of dance injuries. In 1987 NODM also worked closely with the computer company Digital in the presenting of awards for new choreography (these were given to small in-dependent groups as well as more established companies).

New companies

Despite the financial insecurity which faced independent dance groups, new companies continued to emerge throughout the 1980s. Most of them carried on as before, living on social sec-urity, intermittently teaching dance classes and performing in small local venues (with occasional appearances at Dartington, Chisenhale, or at Spring Loaded, The Place's annual season of new dance). A few, however, became very inventive in finding new methods of support. Images, a small group formed by ex-London School of Contemporary Dance students in 1986, man-aged to set up foreign tours before they became well known in Britain, and had the distinction of being the first European, non-classical dance company ever to appear in Pakistan. Another group, La Bouche, went for a slick, almost disco image that was designed to appeal to non-dance audiences – producing music out of their own electronically treated voices and making bright snappy choreography that had the speed and accessibility of pop

49

videos. The Cholmondeleys, a company founded by two students from the Laban Centre in 1984, started out by making short, witty pieces that could be performed in cabarets or at dance halls.

The range of new groups was very wide, and though some groups, like La Bouche, Arc and Images were presenting work that was rooted in fairly conventional modern dance technique, others were following in the political, experimental footsteps of the 1970s. Lloyd Newson, once a performer with Extemporary Dance Theatre, left the security of the company in 1985 to set up his own small group, DV8. Like many choreographers before him, he felt that it was impossible to make the work that interested him while having to conform to the demands of a company's repertoire. He also wanted to create a situation in which dancers and choreographers collaborated on work, rather than the former simply carrying out the latter's instructions. DV8's work is a dramatic exploration of sexual stereotypes, and of the ways in which people dominate and control each other. It challenges the idea of what is acceptable in a dance performance – showing two men embracing each other, for example – and it uses movement that is often aggressive or 'ugly' to get across its message. Newson does not completely avoid dance technique, but he uses it only to make a point – as for example in a duet where he parodies male/female roles in traditional dance. Most of the movement is improvised out of ordinary gestures, acrobatic falls or the simplest of steps. Newson's desire not to identify DV8 as a 'dance' company is further shown by the fact that the group's full name is DV8 Physical Theatre (see pp. 123–126).

The work of The Cholmondeleys is most obviously political in the fact that it is made and performed by four women. It is not overtly feminist but it shows women relating to each other on stage in ways that extend beyond the normal male–female relationships. Just as innovative, however, is their witty and idiosyncratic style of movement and their use of many different dance forms (see pp. 126–130).

Yolande Snaith is a graduate from Dartington who performs either on her own, or with small groups of dancers under the name Dance Quorum. Her work is also concerned with the way women are perceived, both in dance and in real life, and it incorporates a wide range of roles and images, which are very unlike those presented in ballet or mainstream modern dance.

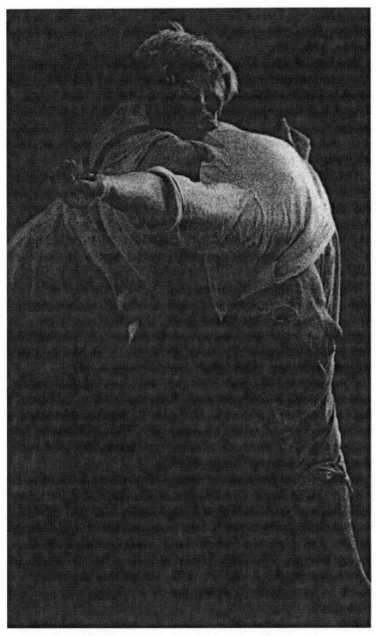

My Sex Our Dance (1986) choreographed and danced by Lloyd Newson and Nigel Charnock. Photo: Eleni Leoussi.

Her background as an art student is also evident in the kind of striking visual effects which she creates with costumes and props (see pp. 130–132).

The use of extraordinary props or unusual collaborations has been another trend among new companies in the late 1980s. For instance Phillipa Donnellan, director of the Vic Vics, made a piece for dancers and accordion players in 1987; Deb Thomas created a work for 'a chorus of huge paper dresses' in the same year, and choreographer Suzanne Watson made work in close collaboration with the video maker Nicola Baldwin.

The 1980s not only saw a new generation of small companies and soloists, it also saw the consolidation of older choreographers and companies. Rosemary Butcher for example, slowly became recognised by a much wider public (performing a sell-out concert at the Queen Elizabeth Hall, London, in 1988) while some of the smaller companies gradually evolved into larger 'middle-scale' companies.

These companies had a more secure and permanent existence than the smaller groups, and some of them received regular funding from the Arts Council, GLAA, GLC etc. They also appeared in more spacious venues (middle-sized theatres) and they presented larger-scale works, with more elaborate costumes and sets, and often with specially commissioned music.

Companies which made this transition from small to middle scale responded in different ways. With a group like Janet Smith and Dancers, the pressure to fill larger theatres brought about a less innovative approach to choreography. The work became less challenging, both in its use of dance movement and in its treatment of subject matter (see pp. 89–92).

In contrast, as Extemporary Dance Theatre became known to a wider public (under the direction of Emilyn Claid), its repertoire became more radical and exploratory (see pp. 92–100). Second Stride, which was a new incarnation of the old group Strider, also presented experimental work in relatively large venues (see pp. 100–116). In this way, many of the ideas and approaches associated with New Dance became accessible to a much wider audience, moving out of the fringe and into the mainstream.

The choreographer who reached the widest audiences of all however, was Michael Clark. Originally a student at The Royal Ballet School, Clark reacted against his background in several

New Puritans (1984) choreographed by Michael Clark. Dancers: Michael Clark and Ellen van Schuylenburch. Photo: Chris Harris.

ways. In 1982 he made his first piece with a small group of dancers – setting classical technique against simple, everyday movements. As his company and productions grew in size he began to create highly theatrical work which debunked the traditional seriousness of the dance performance. Neo-punk rock music, outrageously camp costumes, props and jokes made his work a fashionable cult – appealing to a young, non-specialist audience.

Many aspects of his work do not necessarily conform to the ideas central to the New Dance movement, such as his own over-hyped media image or his rather vague approach to politics (the apparently uncritical use of fascist imagery in *No Fire Escape*

53

in Hell, for example). But like many New Dance choreographers he has continually challenged and subverted sexual stereotypes in his work, and he has done more than anyone to bring radical ideas about dance to the attention of the media and the general public (see pp. 116–122).

Characteristics and Concerns of New Dance

New Dance is not, as Fergus Early and Emilyn Claid pointed out, either a single technique or a single style of movement. It is an alternative way of looking at dance and an attempt to free it from certain constrictions. Yet there are many qualities and many areas of interest that are characteristic of the work produced by independent choreographers, and some of these have become closely associated with the New Dance movement as a whole.

Alternative approaches to movement and choreography

Many dancers and choreographers have come to feel constricted by working inside 'set' techniques like those of classical ballet, Graham or Cunningham. Dancers have argued that rigid systems of training can swamp their personal style and that they may damage themselves by working in a technique that does not come easily to them. Those who lack natural turnout may struggle to cope with the high extensions of ballet or Cunningham while others may find that the Graham technique causes pain in their hip joints. And dancers who do not have the long lean limbs required by the aesthetic of these styles may be made to feel inadequate or ugly. Lea Anderson of The Cholmondeleys, for instance, says that she finds it very painful 'to see dancers struggling to perfect themselves in a style that doesn't suit their bodies' (interview with author, 1988).

These feelings have led many dancers to look for alternative techniques in which to train, even though some may continue using traditional techniques as a base. Some have worked in areas of improvised movement, or with release or contact improvisation; others have explored non-Western techniques like martial arts – and the advantage of all of these forms is not only that they are 'soft' techniques (i.e. do not impose extreme strain on the body) but they do not require years of training.

Similarly, many choreographers have felt that they have nothing left to say with established dance vocabularies and have either looked to alternative forms of movement such as T'ai Chi, or invented their own vocabulary. During the 1970s, for example, many choreographers reacted against the technical virtuosity associated with mainstream dance and began to employ simple, everyday movement in their choreography.

This approach can be seen in the work of Rosemary Butcher, who was influenced by choreographers like Steve Paxton and Yvonne Rainer when she went to America in the early 1970s. In *Uneven Time*, which she made for students in 1974, she used a simple repertoire of runs (in circles, lines and squares), repetitive walks and falls, and gestures which touched the hair and face. The point of the dance was not its 'difficulty' or 'complexity', but the simple shapes formed by the dancers' bodies, the contrast of lightness and weight in their movements and the patterns they made in space.

Richard Alston also adopted this pared-down approach to movement during the mid-1970s when he was working with Fulkerson at Dartington, as did Miranda Tufnell. Tufnell, who performed with Butcher from 1976–82 has spoken of the way in which she tried to free her body of the techniques it had been trained in, and to rediscover her natural style of moving. Her work with Dennis Greenwood, who also performed with Butcher, is made out of very spare gestures and basic actions, like walking and rolling. Gaby Agis, another of Butcher's ex-performers, also reacted against the regimentation of her training at The Place (1977) and went on to create dances that were based on soft, improvised movements.

Many of these choreographers have used release techniques in the training of their dancers and in their own exploration of movement. This is what gives their work its relaxed, weighted quality. Many have also used improvisation (including contact) in both the creation and performance of their work. And many have reacted against the flamboyant dynamic contrasts and varied vocabulary of much mainstream modern dance by restricting themselves to a small range of movement, and repeating phrases, often in long, even sequences.

To audiences used to more elaborate and bravura techniques, this kind of work can look either sloppy or arbitrary. Yet it is usually based on carefully considered ideas. When choreographers discard some of the more traditional points of technique, like stretched limbs and pointed toes, it is often because they are searching for a more natural, more fluid way of moving. When they repeat certain phrases they may be trying to create a hypnotic effect that will imprint the movement upon the viewer's mind. And when they use improvisation it is rarely a matter of letting the dancers do whatever comes into their heads, it is a very structured discipline.

In Butcher's work for example, improvisation is not only crucial to the creation of the movement material, but also to its performance. She starts by giving the dancers a series of practical instructions and images which they use to explore certain kinds of movement (see *Site* and *Imprints* pp. 71–72). As the choreography takes shape, Butcher fixes its structure and spatial design. But within these limits, and the limits of the final range of movement, the dancers are allowed to improvise during every performance. This degree of freedom brings a freshness and a special kind of commitment to the piece, but for the whole process to work properly it can demand as much concentration as remembering 'set' choreography.

Contact improvisation, which might look no more difficult than a spontaneous rough-and-tumble, also demands skill. Like ordinary improvisation it requires the dancers to remain totally aware of each other – ready to respond instantly to what their partner is doing, or bold enough to initiate their own ideas. This is not only demanding for the performers, it can also be exhilarating for the spectators, who see the dancers risking themselves rather than working securely within a set sequence of movements.

Of course some contact improvisation can be a pleasure to do and dull to watch, but with experienced and daring performers it can produce wonderful dance. Kirstie Simson and Julyen Hamilton, who worked together from 1983–87, were as perfectly matched a partnership as, for instance, Anthony Dowell and Antoinette Sibley of The Royal Ballet. They were so closely tuned to each other that they could flip instantly from wild energy (one of them hurling through the air to be caught, on a reflex, by the other) to lyrical tenderness (rolling gently over each other and maintaining an almost caressing contact) to hilarious comedy (ducking out of the way just as the other expects to be caught).

Though much of the choreography associated with New Dance has displayed at least some these characteristics (a release base, a use of simple movement, contact improvisation and repetition) most choreographers have obviously developed their own individual style.

Laurie Booth, for instance, mixes release and contact improvisation with acrobatics and the Brazilian martial art Capoeira – as Mary Fulkerson once said, he 'has virtually invented his own technique' (interview with author, 1985). There are no obvious steps in his dancing but a continual flow of movement, in which his body remains very relaxed. The smooth transitions between his movements are often reminiscent of T'ai Chi. But Booth's weight is rarely in a state of equilibrium, and a slow, fluid phrase of movement might suddenly take a risky dive to the floor, change direction or pause in a dangerous, off-centre balance. He often performs on his own and most of what he does is improvised. But part of the unpredictability and excitement of his performances is that he never hides the fact that he may not know what is going to happen next, that he is always thinking on his feet (see pp. 82–86).

Sue MacLennan, who was taught by Butcher during her second year at Dartington (1969) and performed with her many times, says that she absorbed a great deal from Butcher's work – the use of improvisation to discover movement material, the possibilities of contact and release. But MacLennan's style also reflects her training in more mainstream techniques. Though her dancing is casual and fluid, it can also be fast and energetic, containing detailed, rhythmic footwork, big jumps and high extensions. Sometimes it is so speedy and complicated that it begins to look comic. A limb may shoot off in one direction, while the body spins in another and the head whips round to look – a series of conflicting impulses that looks irresistibly like Billy Whizz (see pp. 76–79).

Lea Anderson of The Cholmondeleys often raids other dance forms for movements and gestures – incorporating ballet, flamenco, ballroom and Scottish folk dance. Sometimes she parodies them, as in *The Clichés and the Holidays* (see p. 126), but often the movements are integrated into her own style, which focuses on detailed, often incongruous movements of the head and hands.

Lloyd Newson, director of DV8, will also use any kind of

movement that he needs to get across his political message. In an interview with the author (1988) he said:

> what is important in dance is people finding a way of moving that is specific to them and allows them to say what they want to say. In DV8 we use the movement we have to use, for example in *Deep End* we did a conventional dance duet, which was necessary as parody, and in *My Sex* Nigel [Charnock] and I did some contact.

Some of the movements can be very violent – with dancers being dropped on the floor, hurling themselves repeatedly against their partners and so on. Some of it is very tender. But the group feel that they have to use extreme physical actions to deal with serious emotions and ideas, and that no single approach to dance can allow them to deal with a full range of subject matter.

Other choreographers have not rejected mainstream techniques so thoroughly, but have coloured them with their own style. Richard Alston, for example, turned away from the simple movement vocabulary he was using around 1974–75 after he had studied with Cunningham in New York. His new style emphasised fast rhythmic footwork and sharply defined movements where the arms, legs and torso might all be working independently of each other. He began to use certain elements from ballet, like classical steps and rounded arms, but he has also retained many of the characteristics of his earlier work – the relaxed open quality which he had learnt from release and T'ai Chi, and the use of weight and partnering he had absorbed from contact improvisation (see *Doublework*, pp. 100–103).

Siobhan Davies's work was also strongly influenced by Cunningham in its curving movements of the torso, high extensions and complex footwork. But she has also developed a distinctive softness and smoothness of style that often incorporates dramatic gestures (see *Carnival* and *Silent Partners*, pp. 108–111) – and in her most recent work has been exploring the extreme fluidity of release.

Michael Clark's work has been influenced both by Cunningham and by his classical training, but his own stamp is unmistakable. A classical *rond de jambe* may be performed with a reckless tilt of the torso; a dancer standing in fourth position may have his or her hips thrust provocatively to one side; beaten jumps may be accompanied by disco arm movements; lifts and rolls may look like moves from contact improvisation. Clark also tends to set his phrases on fast, hard rhythms, with sudden passages of repetition that are very unlike the seamless transitions of ballet. He will also interrupt phrases of dance with provocative gestures – a V-sign, a fascist salute, a spitting motion or a very explicit embrace.

New forms of staging

Choreographers have not only experimented with new forms of movement and new approaches to choreography, they have also looked at different ways of staging their work. During the mid- to late-1970s, several choreographers began to present dance in the plainest possible form, with no music, no set, and with the dancers dressed in practice clothes. At that time people like Butcher and Tufnell wanted to focus purely on movement, and felt that any form of spectacle would distract attention from its own rhythms and images.

Butcher also began to think about ways in which the setting of a dance performance affected the way it was seen, and like several other choreographers, made some of her works for non-theatre venues. In 1977 she put on a series of concerts in London that took place outside the Economist Building in St James', outside the new Museum of London at the Barbican, on the National Theatre Terrace and in Paternoster Square. In the dances which she made for these settings, she explored the difference between seeing movement from a distance and seeing it close up, as well as the contrast between the small scale of the choreography and the monumental size of the surroundings. In another work for the Arnolfini Gallery, Bristol, her dancers were situated in two separate rooms, and the audience moved between them, piecing together the two halves of the dance for themselves.

The massive piece organised by the X6 collective, *By River and Wharf*, also emphasised the relationship between movement and its physical location. By taking the performance out of the theatre and into public spaces the group tried to suggest that dance was not just a remote art form, but a part of everyday life. Some of Jacky Lansley's work with Limited Dance Company also used unusual or outdoor venues, again to try and make the audience look at the movement with fresh and critical eyes.

Choreographers have also experimented with the ways in which set and costume design can elaborate the meaning or visual impact of their work. Sometimes props, sound and lighting effects have become more important than the choreography, as in Tufnell and Greenwood's *Silver*, where the movement works around the manipulation of various props, and where the central effects are created by lights, sound and projected images (see pp. 75–76).

In other works, design elements have been used to indicate character, plot or theme, although they rarely work in the straightforwardly representational way of traditional dance theatre. In Yolande Snaith's *Scared Shirtless* (1987), a huge shirt is suspended from the ceiling to convey the idea of male oppression (see pp. 130–132), while in another work she subverts the image of female glamour by dressing up in a pink corset and dragging a wardrobe around on chains.

In Fergus Early's *Naples* (1978, revised 1982), the stage is cluttered with lines of washing, a real motor scooter and a spaghetti kitchen – all of which contribute to his tongue-in-cheek modernisation of Bournonville's *Napoli* (see p. 94). Much of the wit and subversiveness in Michael Clark's work comes through his even more outrageous use of props and costumes. The outsize platform shoes, aggressive make-up and buttock-revealing romper suits in *New Puritans* make a shocking contrast to the dazzling, sometimes lyrical quality of the movement. And Clark's desire to challenge conventional sexual roles is blatantly evident in the gender-bending outfits worn in *our caca phoney H. our caca phoney H.* (1985), in which Clark himself appears in a white apron, bubble curls wig, bare bottom and giant dildo. The props and costumes in Jacky Lansley's work have also made an important contribution to its political message – like the planks-as-handbags carried by her and Sally Potter, or the juxtaposition of ballgowns with flippers.

Music

There is no single musical trend discernible in the work associated with New Dance, except perhaps a sense of unrestricted choice. Some choreographers have worked with silence, and some have followed the example of Cunningham and Cage in using music as an independent adjunct to the choreography – not setting the movement to the score, but allowing both elements to develop independently. Some have choreographed more directly to music, but the range of sound can be so extreme as to prevent the relationship sounding at all traditional, like Clark's mix of Chopin, bagpipes and rock music in *Pure Pre-Scenes* (1986).

Cross-over with other art forms

During the 1970s and 1980s, many choreographers combined dance with elements from other forms of performance, such as acting, mime, song, cabaret and live music, and other forms of media, like film. Moving Being was the first British company to do this in its mixed-media productions. But a similar trend has been evident in works by choreographers like Jacky Lansley, Fergus Early, Emilyn Claid, Michael Clark and Ian Spink. These people have argued that speech, singing, film and so on can open up new dimensions in their work – not only connecting dance with other forms but also making it accessible to a wider audience. Ian Spink, for example, uses speech in many of his works because he feels it can communicate certain thoughts and feelings more directly than movement (see *New Tactics* and *Bösendorfer Waltzes* p. 111 and pp. 112–114). What makes these cross-overs different from those in musicals, for example, is the wide range of different forms that may be used in one piece, and the speed and unpredictability with which dance might flip into speech or any other activity.

Ballet of the Night, a performance organised by Fergus Early at the first ADMA festival (1977), was particularly eclectic in its use of different forms. It harked back to the early *Ballet de la Nuit*, which was an extravagant spectacle of music and dance performed at the court of Louis XIV. Early's own performance had a similarly nocturnal theme and was composed of a jumble of items, contributed by different people, which ranged from dance to story-telling, from singing to various sound effects. Among them was a dance starting at 12.20 a.m. about night trains; Maedée Duprès singing night songs with Vincent Brown and Julyen Hamilton at 12.40 a.m.; 'Story Time' – with Ian Mackintosh and slides by Geoff White at 3.30 a.m; and on each

Naples (1978, revived 1982), choreographed by Fergus Early. The picture shows the 1982 revival, with Extemporary Dance Theatre. Photo: Doris Haslehurst.

hour Early himself performed a dance in which he explored the sounds he could make with various props. Emilyn Claid describes these:

> 1 a.m. A sheet of metal and a whip. Fergus dressed in a black suit and tap shoes. Sounds created by tapping on and off the corrugated iron and cracking the whip (building to amazing bangs and crashes).

> 3 a.m. A bowl of water, plastic beach sandals, two plastic spades, a toy motor boat. Fergus dressed in a black swimsuit and swimming cap. Sounds created by water splashing, sandals squelching, spades hitting the water and themselves and the motor of the boat.

> 6 a.m. Black umbrella horse with a white face on it, Fergus inside it with Morris bells on his legs. Sounds created by the bells during Morris dance steps. As it was light by this time,

63

Fergus also used the visual image of closing and opening the
umbrella until we could see the whole smiling face.

(*New Dance* No. 3, 1977, p. 13)

(For further description see the rest of Claid's review, also Jan
Murray's piece about the festival in *Time Out*, 9 June 1977.)

Collaborations

Certain works have not just been a matter of introducing elements from other art forms but have been live collaborations
between artists from different disciplines. In Kirstie Simson and
Julyen Hamilton's *Musk:Red* (1983–84), the musician Matthieu
Keijser not only accompanied the dancers on percussion, but also
took a physical role in the action on stage (see pp. 87–89). Many
of Laurie Booth's improvisations have been the joint production
of different performers too, such as his work with Phil Jeck, the
'scratch' DJ, Harry de Witt, a musician who often 'plays' his
own amplified body on stage, and the mime artist Toby
Sedgwick (see pp. 85–86).

Narrative and politics

While choreographers like Butcher have made works with a
purely formal approach to dance, others have used dance
material to create a story, communicate a theme and, most
frequently, present a political message.

As previous chapters have shown, New Dance grew up
against a background of political radicalism. A new generation
was rebelling against the sexual stereotypes, social conventions
and politics of post-war Britain and this radical spirit shaped the
work of independent choreographers like Lansley and Claid.

Much of Lansley and Claid's choreography challenged
received images of women, but an equally radical message was
offered in a duet performed by Timothy Lamford and Julyen
Hamilton at the first ADMA festival that explored male stereotypes. Parts of the choreography were aggressive and acrobatic,
and seemed to reflect traditional male attitudes. Hamilton
jumped into a handstand on a table, walked across it on his hands
and somersaulted off again; a chorus of anonymous 'footballers'

```
12:00 Kate Flatt and Betsy Gregory. Settling in.
12:20 Trains in the Night. Structured by Jill Gale, interpreted by:Helen Crocker,
Joanna Gale, Kiki Gale, Okun Jones, Jessica Loeb, Vincent Meehan, Jennifer Weston.
Tape made by Martin Mayes.
12:30 What the Queen Does at Night
12:40 Maedee Dupres sings night songs with Vincent Brown and Julyen Hamilton
12:50 Dance of the Hours: One O'Clock
1:00 Ian Mackintosh and Suzy Greengrae
1:20 Instruction and training session
1:40 The Louis XIV Stakes Heat 1
1.50 Dance of the Hours Two o'clock
2:00 What the Queen does at Night
2:15 Ian Mackintosh and Jacky Lansley
2:50 Dance of the Hours Three o'clock
3:00 Maedee Dupres with Vincent Brown and Julyen Hamilton
3:15 The Louis XIV Stakes Heat 2
3:30 Story time Ian Mackintosh with slides by Geoff White
3:50 Dance of the Hours Four o'clock
4:00 What the Queen Does at Night
4:15 "Maria Marten - or Murder in the Red Barn" with James Barton, Mary Prestidge, XX
Stefan Szczelkun, Julian Hough
4:50 Dance of the Hours Five o'clock
5:00 Paul Burwell and Friends
5:40 Finals of Louis XIV Stakes
5:45 The Queen presents prizes.
5:50 Dance of the Hours: Six o'clock
6:00 Maedee Dupres, Vincent Brown Julyen Hamilton play morning songs.
Other contributors may include: Craig Givens, Baily Potter, Rose English, Timothy
Lamford, Etheired Brazin, Cosmo Boot, Maryanyn Mankiewiczovska
6:15 Breakfast served in the restaurant.
This programme was typed by the manic American.
```

Programme of events in *Ballet of the Night* (1977).

did a workout; Lamford and Hamilton improvised around fighting movements, and a recruiting song from *O! What a Lovely War!* was played. But at the same time these attitudes were challenged. Lamford read out a passage from Jung which questioned male violence; the footballers offered sliced oranges to the audience, and the aggressive movements were either softened or made to look foolish – for example Lamford and Hamilton

65

performed a ridiculous 'tap stomp' while the footballers started to fight.

Even in the more conservative 1980s, many choreographers have still explored alternative political ground. DV8's work, for example, explores the way in which people oppress each other in sexual and social relations, and rebels against the pretty images of love that are characteristic of more traditional choreography. Michael Clark also attacks sexual stereotypes and has tried to make work which attracts a young, possibly rebellious audience.

Women dancers like Yolande Snaith and The Cholmondeleys do not present an overt feminist message in their work, but nevertheless retain a close connection to sexual politics. Snaith's *Can Baby Jane Can Can?* (1988) presents alternatives to the traditional image of the female dancer (sex object, sylph or androgynous athlete), as she and Kathy Crick explore the roles of young girls, middle-aged matrons, mother figures and workers. The Cholmondeleys have remained an all-woman group because they feel it gives them 'space to make work without falling into all the old heterosexual clichés' (interview with author, 1988).

There is even a kind of political edge to the more formal work of choreographers like Butcher. Their innovations have obviously posed a challenge to traditional ideas of dance, and may provoke audiences to look differently at other aspects of culture and society. At the very least it asks them to be more than passive consumers, unlike much of the cheap digestible entertainment that the age has to offer.

Narrative methods

Works with a theme or message may present their subject in very clear ways, as in DV8's *My Sex, Our Dance* (1986), where the movements performed by two men are clear expressions of love, trust or hostility. But few choreographers associated with New Dance employ the simple stories and characters of classical ballet and of certain modern dance works.

Rather than following an explicit plot or argument, movements, images, props and words are often connected through a process of association. Dancers may take on several, unrelated roles in the same dance, props may acquire different symbolic meanings and the relation of words to movement may be very oblique. Consequently the audience has to decipher the work's meaning for itself, and might often find it difficult to do so. An almost notorious instance of this is Spink's *Bösendorfer Waltzes* (1986), in which scenes from Fokine's ballet *The Firebird* are jumbled up with people confessing their dreams and fantasies on a psychiatrist's couch. Adding to the confusion is a clutter of props (including four grand pianos) which relate, in often obscure ways, to the surrealist movement of the 1920s and 1930s.

Accessibility

The question of making dance 'accessible' has always been an important issue in New Dance and was debated at an early X6 conference in August 1976 (written up in the first issue of *New Dance*, p. 4). The irony is that although the movement has always argued that dance should be brought to a much wider public via open classes, workshops and so on, much of the *choreography* associated with the movement has often seemed obscure and difficult to anyone but specialists.

This is not surprising, since pure dance works, with slow, spare movements are not instantly appealing to people with a taste for bravura technique, a good story, familiar music and colourful costumes. Even works that use more theatrical elements (music, props, speech etc.) may be too obscure or uncomfortable in their subject matter to reach a wide audience.

Few choreographers have actually succeeded in being experimental and popular at the same time. Ian Spink, for example, has frequently been attacked for the difficulty of some of his most innovative works. Those who knew nothing about the historical background to *Bösendorfer Waltzes* were completely baffled by it. And though his next piece, *Weighing the Heart*, was a more directly entertaining work (with copious programme notes to explain the action) Spink still maintains that he is not interested in making his work too simple:

> There are a lot of easy answers being offered in this world, especially on television and in popular entertainment . . . you're told when to feel happy and when to feel sad, and that it's OK because everything finishes up alright in the end.

He feels that his own work 'allows people to go on exploring, everyone can find different things to look at and think about and they can argue about what it all means' (interview with author, 1987).

Janet Smith on the other hand, believes that dance should never appear mysterious and difficult. Most of her works have been accessible to a wide public, with simple themes or stories, vivid costumes and clear attractive movement that has been choreographed directly to the music. Certain critics argue, though, that her concern for simplicity has prevented her from stretching her audience and developing new ideas.

Emilyn Claid created an unusually successful mix of innovation and popular appeal when she took over Extemporary Dance Company in 1981. Though she retained her political commitments and her interest in exploring new styles of movement, she wanted to get away from the specialist, introverted image presented by some of the independent dance groups. She wanted to bring new audiences to dance, not to frighten them away. So while many of the works that she commissioned were boldly experimental, she made sure that they had some kind of immediate appeal. This might be a broad comic streak, a strong narrative, or the kind of music that would appeal to a large, and young, audience. None of these elements compromised her commitment to adventurous dance; they were simply the ingredients of good theatre. This was one reason why the company changed its name under her direction to Extemporary Dance Theatre.

Choreographers and Works

It is impossible to cover all the choreographers who have been associated with, or influenced by, the New Dance movement, and even more impossible to describe all of their works. But this chapter will discuss a few of the most well-known choreographers with reference to central works from the 1970s and 1980s. The choreographers have been arranged into rough groups: Rosemary Butcher and those who have worked with her; Laurie Booth, Kirstie Simson and Julyen Hamilton, much of whose work is based on contact improvisation and the martial arts; middle-scale companies like Extemporary Dance Theatre and Second Stride; and finally four groups of artists who emerged during the 1980s.

Rosemary Butcher

Butcher took ballet classes as a child, and in 1965 went to study at Dartington College. At that time, she was the only full-time dance student at the college and had many opportunities to create her own work. But it was during visits to America (in 1968–69, and again in 1970–72) that she discovered the choreographers who were really to inspire her – Trisha Brown, Yvonne Rainer, Steve Paxton and Elaine Summers.

After America she returned to teach at Dartington, and in 1974 went to Glasgow to work with the Moveable Workshop Dance Company (a group attached to Scottish Ballet). Back in London, she formed a company that included Sue MacLennan (whom she had taught at Dartington), Maedée Duprès and Julyen Hamilton, and gave her first performances in 1976 at the Serpentine Gallery.

The audience for her early work was not, she remembers, 'a specifically dance audience, there were a lot of visual arts people' and their responses varied a lot. Some people saw how carefully her works were designed and constructed (mostly, she thinks, the

69

visual arts audience); others thought the movement was too simple and repetitive, and suggested that her work should be seen in more varied programmes.

One of her most highly regarded pieces was *Landings* (1976), which won her second prize in The Royal Academy of Arts Award; another was *Anchor Relay* (1977) which was performed at Riverside Studios and at Dartington. This was structured like a relay race, with the dancers falling and picking each other up in constant motion. It was so well received that Butcher was given an Arts Council grant of £7000 and appointed Resident Choreographer at Riverside Studios for two years.

What should have been a good period for Butcher turned out to be disastrous, however. Duprès and Hamilton left shortly afterwards to dance with Richard Alston, who was by that time a much more established choreographer, and Butcher was left with a group of inexperienced dancers. Her choreography had also, by this time, become quite rarefied. The movement was even more minimal, there was no music and everything was done in 'real' rather than theatrical time (i.e. letting each movement happen at its own speed, rather than artificially speeding it up or slowing it down to create a dramatic effect). As a result Butcher received very poor reviews, and the *Daily Telegraph* and *Guardian* critics went so far as to say that her work should be stopped because it was putting audiences off seeing other experimental dance.

Few of Butcher's critics perceived that this work was simply a stage in her development – that like a painter or a sculptor she was experimenting with how far she could strip her choreography down to its barest essentials. No one stopped to think that she would probably then develop in other directions. Instead, all of her supporters thought that they had made a mistake and her grant was replaced by a much smaller one.

However Butcher carried on working, and her choreography began to develop. Pieces made in collaboration with other well-known artists, like composer Michael Nyman and sculptor Heinz-Dieter Pietsch, attracted a wider audience, and gradually her work won greater recognition. In 1986 a series of performances was held at the Riverside Studios to celebrate ten years of her choreography; and in the following year she was not only given a substantial grant from the Arts Council but she also began to develop some of her work for television.

Butcher's work is not only admired in its own right, but is also recognised as a major influence on other choreographers, particularly those who have performed her work like Miranda Tufnell, Dennis Greenwood, Sue MacLennan and Gaby Agis.

Important work

Landings (1976)
Choreography: Rosemary Butcher. *Music:* Alan Lamb.

This was a duet for Duprès and Hamilton which was based on ideas of falling and being caught, on suspending and dropping weight, on balancing and then letting go, principles that Butcher had absorbed back in the 1960s via the work of Doris Humphrey (see Glossary). There were moments of quiet communication between the dancers, when one softly touched the back of the other's neck as a signal for them both to run forward together. But there were also moments of great daring, when one dancer balanced in a high extension and slowly tilted sideways while the other ran across the stage to come and break the fall. A lot of the movement was improvised in performance, though the structure of the piece was very carefully set. Butcher also made strong use of contrast in the movement: moments of stillness would happen at the same time as high energy activity, and one dancer would echo the shape of the other dancer, before going on to make a completely different kind of movement.

Site (1983)
Choreography: Rosemary Butcher. *Music:* Malcolm Clark.
Design: Heinz-Dieter Pietsch.

The ideas for this piece were related to memory (sifting the past) and to the physical actions of archaeologists, so the initial movement instructions which Butcher gave her dancers were involved with sifting, digging and scraping, with curling up the body (as if burying it) and with picking up on what the other dancers were doing.

Heinz-Dieter Pietsch created a floor sculpture which was a rectangle of ragged paper pulp lit by another rectangle of neon lights, and Malcolm Clark composed a score of threatening rumbles and distant machine noises.

During the piece, the three dancers made their way very slowly around the sculpture, pausing to let their feet rasp against the rough paper, to roll carefully over the lights or to warm their hands against them. Tentatively they would copy each other or seem to experiment with their own physical powers, stretching out their limbs, dropping their bodies to the floor and exploring the stage. Sometimes they squinted against the glare of the overhead stage lights, apparently listening to the music, which droned like an overhead plane. Though the movement ideas were very practical, the atmosphere of the piece was very dramatic, creating a sense of people discovering themselves as well as being threatened by what was outside them.

Imprints (1983)
Choreography: Rosemary Butcher. *Music:* Malcolm Clark.
Design: Heinz-Dieter Pietsch.

The idea for this piece came from a site in East London which Pietsch and Butcher discovered during a walk. It was a run-down street with long stretches of corrugated iron masking demolition sites, and at one point there was a gap in the iron, showing the crumbling remains of a building behind it.

Pietsch made a sculpture for the piece which imitated that image, in which two grey ragged-edged screens stood side by side, a few inches apart, in a pool of light. The physical tasks which the two dancers worked with were related to leaving and entering different areas of space, and finding ways of 'imprinting' their bodies onto each other and onto the screens.

The dancers circled the stage, moving between light and shadow, and sometimes slipping behind the screens so that their outlines appeared in silhouette. They rarely touched each other, but one of them would pause in a certain position, allowing the other to come and fit his/her body around it before moving on.

With the addition of music by Malcolm Clark that sounded like wind and rain, the piece began to communicate strong feelings of loneliness. The two dancers seemed like ghosts who were haunting an old building, restlessly on the move but trying to hang on to brief moments of communication with their surroundings and with each other.

Flying Lines (1985)
Choreography: Rosemary Butcher. *Music:* Michael Nyman.
Design: Peter Noble.

This was a piece based on ideas associated with flying and gravity, in which the design consisted of trellises, hung with flutter-
ing rags, that were suspended, like kites, from the ceiling.

It began with two dancers sitting on the ground and arching
their bodies upwards as if being tugged by the wind. Suddenly
they broke into a fast curving run as if they had broken free from
gravity and were soaring through space. The next section was a
solo danced by Butcher herself in which the same ideas were
repeated on a much smaller scale. She crouched down to the
floor and then rose softly on to her toes to suggest the alternating
downward pull of gravity and uplift of the wind.

In the long final section seven or eight dancers filled the stage,
sometimes running together, sometimes taking it in turns to join
in. They ran in lines and circles, often going backwards and
coming close to colliding, like kites in danger of getting tangled
with each other. In some passages they moved very fast, holding
out their arms or whipping them backwards like streamers flying
in the wind, and they twisted and dipped their bodies as if
caught on eddying currents of air. In others, they moved much
slower, sinking down to the floor as if the wind had suddenly
dropped.

The effect of these repetitive runs and dips was to create a
hypnotic and exhilarating sense of freedom. And this was
emphasised by the repeating chord sequences of Nyman's piano
music, which, though composed independently of the movement, had the same sense of energy and spaciousness.
Appropriately, Butcher's own solo was danced in silence.

Touch the Earth (1987)
Choreography: Rosemary Butcher. *Music:* Michael Nyman.
Design: Heinz-Dieter Pietsch.

The ideas behind this piece were connected with territory and
loss of land, and were partly associated with the displacement of
the North American Indians. It was first performed at the
Whitechapel Gallery in London and the long thin space was
enclosed by Pietsch's set – roughly woven paper, steel screens

and clusters of poles that suggested, among other things, spears, tools or the skeletons of wigwams.

Butcher began the piece by laying out sticks all round the dance area, almost as an act of territorial possession. Other dancers joined in, making gestures that suggested working the land and worshipping the gods of earth and sky. Increasingly, a sense of a community developed, with dancers walking together and sharing similar movements. Spatially, the piece seemed to work in layers, with certain dancers moving in the foreground while others remained in the background, either echoing their gestures, or standing still.

Towards the end the community seemed to be breaking up: groups began to splinter, the movements slowed down as if the dancers were exhausted, and everyone began to run backwards and forwards as if they were being threatened by an outside force. Finally the dancers drifted towards the back as if expelled from the protection of their homeland.

Nyman's music consisted of high repetitive melodies performed by women's voices and strings, and it matched the choreography perfectly in the way that musical patterns were built out of a few simple themes, and in the way it communicated a strong sense of passion and loss.

Miranda Tufnell and Dennis Greenwood

Dennis Greenwood began dancing seriously when he entered the London School of Contemporary Dance in 1968. He joined Alston's group Strider in 1971 and then, after a break of two years when he thought he 'had had enough of moving', he started to work with Butcher.

Tufnell was a student at The Place from 1973–75, ('escaping from the academic confines of university'), and in 1975 she went to New York with Eva Karczag and Richard Alston. Like Alston she became very interested in the Cunningham technique, but was even more absorbed by the idea of using basic elements of movement. She studied the Alexander technique (which is like release in that it aims to free the body from bad postural habits and to rediscover a natural way of moving). She started to try and throw off the technical dance movements that had been 'drilled into her body' during her training. These seemed to her 'to be clichés' that got in the way of her own movement style. For several years Tufnell also performed with Rosemary Butcher, before going on to make work with Greenwood.

Tufnell and Greenwood's work is not unlike Butcher's in its use of simple, often improvised movement, in its building up of clear formal patterns and in its use of 'real' rather than 'theatrical' time. But what is most distinctive about it are the images which are created through lighting effects, sound and props. Because of this element, some critics have argued that their work is not 'dance' and they have found it harder to survive than most other independent choreographers, receiving minimal funding and review space during the course of their career.

They rarely work with other dancers (though Merry Dufton performed in *Silver*) partly because they have never been able to afford to pay anyone, but partly because it keeps them 'small enough for both of [them] to really make a contribution, without the whole thing getting chaotic' (all quotes from interview with author, 1985).

Important work

Silver (1984)
Choreography: Miranda Tufnell, Dennis Greenwood.
Sound: Anna Lockwood, Bob Bielechi (sound ball).
Design: Miranda Tufnell, Dennis Greenwood.

A world of uncertainty was created in this work through extra-ordinary combinations of light and shadow, movement and still-ness, sound and silence. The choreography was minimal, geared simply towards travelling and handling the props.

The stage was dimly lit, full of white shrouded furniture that cast large shadows. The two dancers made their way slowly round it, pausing occasionally to echo each other's movements or to fit their limbs around the angle of a chair or table. It became increasingly difficult to tell the difference between the dancers and the furniture, particularly when a series of slide pro-jections cast patterns of light and shadow onto the whole stage, sometimes dissolving it into watery lines like a river, or casting dark shapes like a thick forest.

Sound was also used to play tricks with the audience's percep-tions. A speaker concealed in a black ball was swung across the stage, creating an arc of sound that cut through a beam of light. The ball was then placed behind a bowl of water. Light was projected through the water casting rippling shadows onto the ball, and at the same time, sounds of running water came from the speaker. One bowl of water was real, but the black ball had been transformed into another one by the use of these simple but effective devices.

Sue MacLennan

After studying ballet as a child, MacLennan went to Dartington in 1968 and was one of the first dancers to work with Butcher on her final return from the United States. For a long time she felt no desire to choreograph, because 'Rosemary uses your own creative input so much' (interview with author, 1987), and she admits that her first impulse to make work came partly from outside pressure – 'there was a lot of feeling in the New Dance world at that time that everyone should be a choreographer, that you weren't quite worthy if you just danced for someone else.'

MacLennan says that her first works were very influenced by Butcher but she slowly developed her own idiosyncratic style. Her first major piece, *Interruptions*, was made in 1981 for herself, Kirstie Simson, Gaby Agis and Craig Givens. It was constructed in sections, each one exploring a different movement idea, and it was also very funny. She recalls that 'It began with Kirstie sitting on a chair chanting "Red lorry yellow lorry"' (accompanied by manic gestures) 'and when we took it to the Dartington Festival I was afraid we'd be lynched for being ridiculous, but every one loved it.'

The starting point of MacLennan's works is usually very specific – a particular movement, a rhythm or some kind of visual image. (In *Seven Desperate Years* (1984), she used images of the wild west from a story about Billy the Kid. These images became the basis for developing some of the movement although the dance itself did not attempt to recreate the plot.)

Many of her works are episodic, with one section stringing onto the next rather than evolving into a whole. For example she made one piece that was constructed around the different sounds and rhythms that could be produced by dancing in tap

Programme for Sue MacLennan's *Interruptions* (1981).

shoes. Different sections involved tapping on and off concrete; hanging from a lighting bar and tapping against the wall, and tapping against a radiator.

MacLennan has become a respected choreographer and performer, though her most successful works have tended to be solos, and she has not formed a permanent company. However when she does choreograph with other dancers, she works closely with them – often leaving it up to them to improvise with the ideas she has suggested. She also frequently collaborates with composers such as Stephen Montague and, more recently, visual artists such as David Ward.

Important work

New Moves (1983)
Choreography: Sue MacLennan. *Music:* John King.
Costumes: Johanna Agis.

Made on inexperienced as well as professional dancers, this was a strictly episodic work that involved complicated rhythms. One passage was based on a very tricky count of twos and threes (the dancers even moved their faces to this rhythm). Another passage had the dancers walking in single file around the space, then stopping suddenly, each of their heads snapping round in turn. As this continued one or two dancers stepped out of line and pushed in front of someone else, improvising movement variations. Other sections were based on moving forwards and backwards, on skipping and jumping – each one a clear statement of a new and self-contained movement theme.

Gravity Is Proving Most Difficult (1984)
Choreography: Sue MacLennan. *Music:* Stephen Montague,
Ian Mitchell. *Costumes:* Sara Easby.

This piece started with MacLennan's idea that she wanted to make a piece about little fingers, because 'they were the most neglected area in dance'. She then started to think about contrasts between tiny movements (a gesture with a little finger) and very large ones. In the final work both dance and music veered between two extremes building up to high volume, speed and size, and paring down into moments of quiet stillness.

Against Interpretation (1986)
Choreography: Sue MacLennan. *Music:* William Schottstaedt.
Design: David Ward.

This piece was made in close collaboration with visual artist

David Ward, so that the images made by the dancer (MacLennan herself) were created in relation to the lighting, costumes and props. The piece began with a visual flourish, a sense of MacLennan being on public display. Dressed in a red party frock and strappy silver shoes she was seated beside a floor-to-ceiling swathe of red velvet. But this glamorous image contrasted oddly with the privacy of her actual movements. At first she simply sat still, listening to a personal stereo, then she moved onto a stool where she sat and moved only her arms. She clutched her elbow in the palm of her other hand and thrust it into the air; then using the same clutching gesture she began to use her hands to explore her face and her body. There was something awkward and constricted about her actions that made you question why she was sitting there and what she was feeling, and that sense of uncertainty remained haunting even when she began to move more freely around the stage.

Gaby Agis

Gaby Agis first went to dance classes at her local comprehensive school where she was taught by Rosemary Butcher. In 1977 she was accepted at The Place, but left after a year, having disliked the strictness of the teaching, as well as its strong emphasis on Graham technique. From 1981–84 she performed with Butcher's company, developing the intensely inward presence that is special to her as a performer. During this time she also worked with other choreographers like Michael Clark (*Parts I–IV*) and Sue MacLennan, and in 1983 began to create her own work.

Agis's use of simple improvised movement is very similar to Butcher's, though in her collaborations with sculptor Kate Blacker she has created a powerful contrast between the softness of the dancers' movements and the harshness of the iron structures assembled by the latter. In *Surfacing* (1984) the dancers began by hurling bits of metal around, making a terrifying din before moving on to perform more serene rolls, runs and turns. In another piece designed specially for the Cornerhouse Gallery, Manchester, Blacker created an entire scrap metal environment, lining the gallery ceiling with it, and placing free-standing chunks of it around which the dancers moved.

An important part of Agis's choreography is the sense of communication and trust conveyed by the dancers, who often touch and caress each other. This is particularly true of the all-women dances she has created, which although not intended as feminist statements, have a very strong emphasis on the relations between women.

Although Agis has received some support from the Arts Council, and has reached a wide public with her appearance in *Hail the New Puritan* (a television film about Michael Clark) and her own television dance *Free Fall*, some critics feel that her best work has been done with Butcher's company.

Important work

Undine and the Still (1985)
Choreography: Gaby Agis. *Music:* Ana da Silva.
Design: Graca Cout.

Both set and music contributed to the soft, organic quality of this work. The former was a mound of sand shaped with strongly female curves, and the continuous hypnotic pulse of the latter was reflected in the cyclical repetitive movement. The choreography contained simple rolls, runs and walks, and the dancers were constantly picking up on what the others were doing, imitating each other, returning to familiar movements, and coming together in a unison that looked so relaxed it seemed unplanned.

Ashley Page

Rosemary Butcher also had a strong, if much less predictable influence on the choreographer Ashley Page, who is also a principal dancer with The Royal Ballet. When he first started making dances, Page knew very little about either modern dance or the work associated with New Dance, but he felt that he needed to learn about these unfamiliar kinds of choreography if he was really going to understand the art of creating dances.

Consequently he went to see Ballet Rambert, Michael Clark and nearly all of the performances at the 1983 Dance Umbrella – including a piece by Butcher. He remembers 'loving it, and being transfixed by the way the dancers [Agis and Greenwood] performed. I just wanted to learn how to do it' (interview with author, 1985).

David Gothard at Riverside Studios organised a meeting between Page and Agis, and the next year they collaborated on a

Undine and the Still (1985) choreographed by Gaby Agis. Dancers: Gaby Agis and Helen Rowsell. Photo: Dee Conway.

81

duet for the 1984 Umbrella, *Between Public Places*. This was very much closer to Agis's natural style of moving than Page's – a dialogue created out of touch and intense eye contact which involved a fluid succession of curving, sinking, swaying and dragging movements.

This duet proved to be the critical hit of the Umbrella, a success repeated the following year by *This Is What, Where* (1985) in which there was more of a contrast between Page's classical jumps and high extensions and Agis's softer and more introverted style.

After this, Page went on to work in a much more virtuoso style, combining the classical vocabulary in which he was trained with elements from the Cunningham technique. However there is a quality of softness and stillness that sometimes shows through in his work which clearly relates to Agis's and Butcher's influence.

Laurie Booth

Booth first studied dance at Dartington, though his initial reason for taking the dance theatre course was his interest in 'physical theatre' (see Glossary). During the three years at college (1976–79) he also became involved with X6, one of the first students from Dartington to do so.

After graduating Booth worked briefly with Rosemary Butcher, and with various community dance and theatre projects such as Ludus, Welfare State, Triple Action Theatre and the Cardiff Laboratory Theatre. Even as a student, however, he was interested in making his own work. The performance he gave at the first ADMA festival showed his two main interests at that time. The first was pure contact improvisation, which was further developed when he co-founded the contact group Transitional Identity. The second was his solo work, which gave direct expression to his own thoughts and feelings, and in which dance was interwoven with speech and the manipulation of various props.

In these, as in his later works, Booth improvised heavily with his material. Usually the sense of chance and discovery adds an edge of excitement to his work, though at worst it can prevent him from presenting his ideas clearly and succinctly enough.

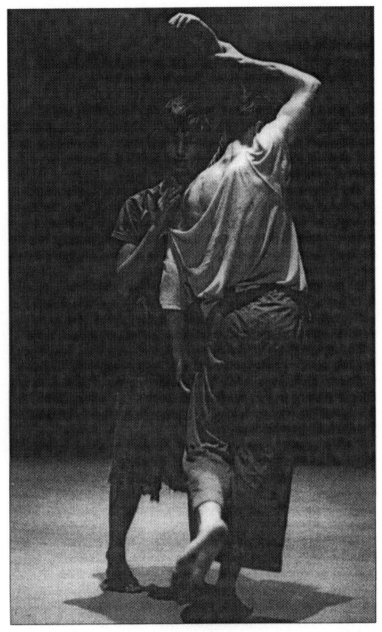

Between Public Places (1984). Choreographed and performed by Gaby Agis and Ashley Page. Photo: Peter Sayers.

83

Important work

Animal Parts (1984)
Choreography: Laurie Booth. *Film and music:* Plumelia Hairart.
Lighting design and visual effects: Steve Whitson.

This was a full-length work, which used dance, film, slides, live music and numerous props. Its subject was man's treatment of animals, and the stage was littered with furry and rubbery toy pets that represented the sentimentalised and commercial attitudes of a consumer society.

The piece started out with Booth performing a solo dance, a playful sequence of rolls, falls, slides and balances. Then, halfway through, he began to tell a story about a group of animals who lived in a strip of fertile desert, having used their intelligence to get away from the destructive behaviour of man. Hairart played some loud music at the side of the stage.

As he spoke, Booth's dancing started to reflect parts of the story (imitating a monkey with a hangover) and the things he said began to reflect his movement (debating aloud how to move on from a particularly tangled position he had got himself into).

During the piece he also narrated two other stories. In the first he took on the character of a farmer trying to justify his brutal treatment of chickens, while behind him a series of slides showed animals undergoing vivisection, or shut up in battery farms. In the second he was an animal at a zoo talking about the frustrations of being stuck in a cage.

During another section he and Hairart watched a scratch video of news items and adverts, showing man's aggressive behaviour to innocent people, and suggesting that the way we treat animals is part of a more general kind of violence. During certain sections Hairart played loud abrasive and uncomfortable electronic music.

The piece was uncomfortable in other ways too. Many of the slides were upsetting to look at (some people walked out), there was no interval during the one-and-three-quarter hours, and there was a deliberately unpolished quality about the slides, the video and the music. Booth often tries to upset his audience in an effort to make them think, however. He is less interested in producing entertainment that people can sit back and enjoy than in getting to their consciences.

Mercurial States (1987)
Choreography: Laurie Booth. *Sound score:* Phillip Jeck.
Design: Andrzej Borkowski. *Drawings:* Ian Pollock.

This was made in collaboration with the mime artist Toby
Sedgwick, and was based on a short story by G. K. Chesterton
about two men who try to create a language based entirely on
movement. Interestingly, the discipline of working within a specific story forced Booth into working in an unusually clear,
entertaining and economical way.

The story had a kind of symbolic meaning in that the two
men became increasingly indifferent to the conventions of
society as they developed their own strange and private world of
language. Society was represented by three 'stern sisters' (in
reality three tailor's dummies) who 'watched' in disapproval as
the two men evolved their own purely physical mode of conversation. Their movements were in fact uncannily like speech, even
though they didn't use obvious mime. A restless tapping of the
fingers was like a low muttering, little jerks of the head were like
question marks, and as they became more fluent they rolled and

Animal Parts (1984). Choreographed and danced by Laurie Booth. Photo: Peter
Sayers.

85

cantered round each other in long passages of 'dialogue', picking up on each other's movement, often through improvisation.

The piece also used slide projections and lighting effects to show the different moods and different stages in the two men's relationship. Particularly powerful was the circle of cartoon figures which were drawn by Ian Pollock and which, with the accompaniment of taped shouts and abuse, seemed to threaten and argue with the two rebellious men.

Kirstie Simson and Julyen Hamilton

Like Booth, Simson and Hamilton have based their choreography on contact improvisation and the martial arts, sometimes performing straight contact duets, sometimes creating work that weaves together dance, music, speech and a complicated array of props.

Hamilton was closely involved with the development of New Dance from early on in his career. He first started dancing with the Cambridge Contemporary Dance Group, and after leaving university he took up a place at London School of Contemporary Dance. In 1976 he started performing with London Contemporary Dance Theatre, but became more interested in what was happening on the independent dance scene. He performed with Rosemary Butcher, Tim Lamford, and Mary Fulkerson and then in 1977 worked with Richard Alston, creating one of the roles in *Doublework*. He also gained a reputation as a brilliant teacher, and in 1980 moved to Amsterdam where he taught at the Theatreschool. He performed in Pauline de Groot's Dancegroup and worked with artists from other disciplines as a member of Bearegingstone Studio.

Simson's interest in movement developed out of sports, and took her to the Laban Centre when it was still at Addlestone, Surrey. From 1978–79 she worked with Rosemary Butcher, and it was at this time that she learnt the basis of improvisation and contact – approaches to dancing which suited her much better than the more formalised technique which she had studied at Laban (see Jann Parry's article on Simson, *Dance Theatre Journal* 4:1 Spring 1986, pp. 4–5). But she really started to discover her own way of moving when she took Steve Paxton's classes at the Dartington Festival in 1980. Equally important for her was the

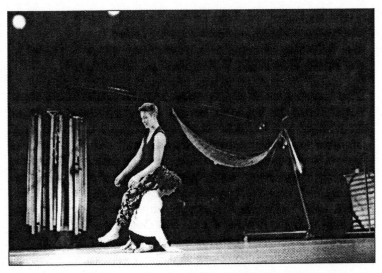

Kirstie Simson and Julyen Hamilton in *Musk:Red* (1983). Photo Eleni Leoussi.

discovery of Ki Aikido, a martial art form that develops strength and concentration through breathing techniques.

Around this time she became involved with Transitional Identity – performing and 'jamming' with Laurie Booth, Anna Furse, Claire Hayes, Gaby Agis and Sue MacLennan. In 1983 she went to New York where she performed with Steve Paxton and Nancy Stark Smith and then went to Amsterdam where she started working with Hamilton. The duo were very well received in Holland, but in England they never achieved the wide recognition they deserved. They stopped working together in 1987.

Important work

Musk:Red (1983–84)
Choreography: Kirstie Simson, Julyen Hamilton.
Music: Matthieu Keijser. *Design for mobile:* Henny van Belkam.

This was made in collaboration with the percussionist Matthieu Keijser. A programme note for its performances at 1984's Dance Umbrella stated that the piece was about the 'development of performance possibilities which exist between music and dance'. The point was not just to have music accompanying dance, but

87

to have musicians and dancers improvising together, sharing what they were doing, or disrupting each other.

The following description is taken from my own review in *Dance Theatre Journal* (2:1 Winter 1983, pp. 30–31).

The stage is packed with instruments and objects. Giant-sized wind chimes are balanced on one end of a huge silver crane by a bright red oil drum; there is a complicated arrangement of silver and red percussion instruments, and a number of brown carrier bags, all half covered in red paint. Keijser plays a steady drum beat, while Simson very carefully begins to arrange the bags in descending order of size and then puts them one inside the other. At the centre of the stage, Hamilton dances a solo of balancing and falling, in which he makes tiny gestures with his hands and head, like a private conversation in sign language.

Keijser looks ready to interfere. He starts playing a brass gong, moving closer to Hamilton and playing more and more loudly. In response, Hamilton's movements get bigger and bigger until he falls to the floor and is rolled round and round by the unbearable noise. Simson has by now put all the bags together; she quietly puts a large red paint bush into the inside bag and takes the gong away from Keijser. The relief of silence is immense.

When Simson dances her own solo she echoes Hamilton in the way she catches her weight in balances, then lets it drop, though she has a much more acrobatic way of diving or rolling to the floor and changing direction with dangerous bursts of speed. At first Keijser simply accompanies her, then he starts treating her like one of his instruments, playing over the surface of her body with drumsticks and gradually forcing her into the middle of the cage of windchimes, which he then starts playing. Later on, the windchimes are dismantled, littering the stage like felled logs, and Simson plays games of balancing on them. Throughout the piece instruments are always being turned into props, obstacles and toys like this.

In the final section, Simson and Hamilton perform a contact duet though it is not just a game of catching each other's weight and maintaining close connection. It is also a game of avoidance as they swerve, drop and fall out of each other's way with mounting wildness and hysteria. Again Keijser decides to take control of the situation. He starts propelling the crane towards the two dancers, but the wind chimes are no longer attached to one end, and in their place is a mobile of hanging pots and pans. As the crane comes closer Simson and Hamilton get tangled up with the pans, ducking to avoid them, but also bumping and clanging against them as if they were extra percussion instruments.

Janet Smith and Dancers

Janet Smith studied dance and drama at Dartington College from 1969–71. After gaining her teacher's certificate in 1972 from Rolle College, Devon, she went to New York to get a wider experience of dance. 'Everyone,' she says, 'wanted to go, there was so little modern dance over here' (*Dance Theatre Journal* 1:3, 1983 p. 17). Once in America she studied with Dan Wagoner and Viola Farber, with teachers from the Cunningham Studio and at the Joffrey School of Ballet. But it was Erick Hawkins who was to have the greatest influence on her. He taught her to be aware of the dynamics of music and to bring these out in her choreography, and his soft, fluid style can be seen in much of Smith's own work. Unlike many recent choreographers, Smith still tends to work very closely with music, tying her movement to its phrasing rather than keeping the two elements separate; much of her work has been made in close collaboration with composers, such as Christopher Benstead.

When she returned to England in 1974, Smith began a series of dance performances with the musician/composer Gordon Jones, which they toured in colleges, schools and theatres throughout the country. In 1975 she became attached to Trinity and All Saints College in Leeds, where she taught and choreographed, and it was in Leeds too that, in 1976, she founded the Janet Smith Dance Group with funds from Yorkshire Arts.

When she and her company appeared at the ADMA festival in 1977, her work was noticeable for its high standard of performance, its wit and accessibility – qualities that became the company's hallmarks.

Jan Murray described a performance at the Battersea Arts Centre later that year as follows:

The Man Who Painted the Sun (subtitled 'Sketches from the Life of Vincent van Gogh') was fascinatingly accompanied by a trio of musicians on percussion instruments (some of which were *objets trouvés*) and oriental wind instruments . . . The piece was long (close to half an hour) and divided into scenes which explored different periods of the painter's life – some of these were accompanied by live readings from his diaries. The movement, as always with Janet, was marvellously fluid. Her vocabulary is relatively limited, but she knows how to bring out the best in her cast (four women), and varied her approach for each short scene.

Fence . . . was sheer delight – fast funny and inventive. Four women and a man formed every conceivable type of fence with their bodies, and accompanied themselves with snatches of conversation ('Can I borrow a cup of sugar?' asked one, leaning his elbow on the 'fence') and amusing self-manufactured sound effects. A wonderful piece for a children's programme.

(From an unpublished report for the Arts Council, 1977)

Though Smith could not afford to run a permanent company when she first began making work, by 1982 she had established a middle-scale company with around six or seven full-time members. That year also saw the first of her extensive foreign tours, which have often been funded by the British Council, and in 1984 she was given a revenue grant (regular annual funding) by the Arts Council.

Smith's works frequently contain some kind of narrative, and even when they are abstract they are always easily approachable. Unlike choreographers who challenge their audiences with very pedestrian or even deliberately ugly movements, Smith's style has always been very easy on the eye, using movement that is clear, well crafted and rhythmic, with graceful arms, sweeping curves of the leg, and legible dramatic gestures.

Initially Smith choreographed all the works herself, though she later began to incorporate works by Christopher Bruce and Robert North into her programmes. Virtually all of her pieces have a human element which the audience can hold on to – a situation, a set of characters or a story. Although certain critics have argued that Smith has failed to experiment with enough different ideas, for a long time her company had huge popular

Square Leg (1976, revived 1981), choreographed by Janet Smith. Dancers: Gill Clarke and Nicholas Burge. Photo: Dee Conway.

support. (In the summer of 1988, however, the company found itself in such acute financial difficulties that it had to disband.)

Important work

Square Leg (1976, revived 1981)
Choreography: Janet Smith. *Tape:* Christopher Benstead.

This, like so much of Smith's work, was a very English piece, a witty parody of a cricket match. The dancers were dressed in

91

impeccable 'whites' and their movements started out as an almost straightforward mime of batting, bowling and catching (accompanied by a frantic BBC commentary). The movement developed into a more stylised form of dancing with the cricket gestures being incorporated into long phrases of movement. Finally it moved into a style that was completely, and hilariously removed from cricket: for example, the dancers performed swings of the leg that were straight out of Japanese martial arts.

There has always been a strong sense of the past in Smith's work, as in *Until the Tide Turns* (1980), which was based on photographs of Whitby fishing folk in the nineteenth century; or *Another Man Drowning* (1983), which was inspired by the paintings of L. S. Lowry; or the more recent *Still No Word from Anton* (1986).

Still No Word from Anton (1986)
Choreography: Janet Smith. *Music:* Christopher Benstead.
Design: Gill Longton.

This was based on the radio soap operas of the 1950s and was set to a sharp and funny mix of radio extracts, adverts and incidental music. Some of the movement parodied the absurd simple-mindedness of the stories, using comic-strip gestures of passion and heartache. But some of it also developed into more elaborate choreographic fantasies, as in the suicidal car ride which had one of the dancers swooping and colliding through the air on the shoulders of two men; or the sequence of marital crises which turned duets and trios into a tangle of cleverly botched lifts and misplaced partners. This was very funny and inventive choreography, having a slightly sharper edge and more abrupt rhythms than much of Smith's work.

Extemporary Dance Theatre

When the company was founded by Geoff Powell in 1975 it was called Extemporary Dance Company, and was intended only to last for the duration of that summer's Edinburgh Festival. However, the dancers (all students from London School of Contemporary Dance) received such good reviews that they decided to continue working on a full-time basis. Their aim was to bridge the gap between the larger dance companies – who performed in major towns and cities – and small experimental companies (like Rosemary Butcher's) whose work appealed to specialist audiences. They toured round Britain, appearing in small venues. Though the style of their work was often a scaled-down version of London Contemporary Dance Theatre, the company commissioned work from a sufficiently wide range of choreographers (including Micha Bergese and Janet Smith) to give Extemporary's programme a distinctive image.

In 1978 Paul Taras, a former principal with Ballet Rambert, took over the direction of the company. He introduced works by more prestigious choreographers (including Richard Alston and Robert North) and also encouraged company members to choreograph pieces of their own. But by 1981 the company's general Graham/ballet-based style was beginning to look stale, and the repertoire was not reflecting the kinds of experiment which had taken place in dance during the late 1970s. So a new director was appointed, the company was renamed, and a new image emerged.

Taras' successor was Emilyn Claid, who started to build up a new repertoire that was both challenging and experimental, but also accessible to a wide public. New choreographers such as Michael Clark, Karole Armitage and Fergus Early were brought in, and the emphasis shifted from pure dance to a more theatrical image – hence the company's new name – Extemporary Dance Theatre.

In response to these developments, the dancers in the company began to change. Some left, some new ones arrived, some of the old ones developed new skills, and in a short space of time the company turned into a group of unusually individual performers, whose distinctive skills and personalities were all made good use of in the new repertoire.

Important work (1981–85)

Among Claid's early commissions were *12XU* (1983) a love duet for two men by Michael Clark in which classically-based movement was set to hard aggressive punk music, and Fergus Early's *Naples* which was based on an earlier piece made for X6 in 1978 (see *New Dance* No. 9, 1978 p. 11 for description).

Naples (1982)

Choreography: Fergus Early. *Music:* Simon Holger Paulli,
Edvard Helsted, Niels Gade. *Design:* Craig Givens.

This piece was a twentieth-century spoof of the last act of
Napoli, the great Romantic ballet by the Danish choreographer
Bournonville. Early ignored the main story, and in place of
the fishing village scenes he portrayed a twentieth-century
fantasy about Naples. A cast of quarrelsome characters cooked
spaghetti, listened to football and showed off their Lambrettas,
and mixed up in this portrayal of everyday life (and cliché) were
echoes of Bournonville's choreography (and sometimes, like the
Pas de six, whole chunks of it). It was both an affectionate re-
interpretation of the original ballet and also a comedy in its own
right – Lloyd Newson rolling his eyes and slicking back his bril-
liantined hair as the spivvy ice cream salesman was particularly
funny.

Counter Revolution (1981)

Choreography: David Gordon.

The American David Gordon created three very successful
works with the company. In *Counter Revolution* (1981), the
dancers began by talking through their every action, making a
kind of musical accompaniment out of their words – 'step-slide-
cross-open-lie-sit-and-stand' etc. They were also labelled with
numbers, and whole sections of the piece involved complex
mathematical games. For instance, as they danced, the performers called out their own numbers, then everyone had to run and
stand in the correct order that spelled out the sum of all their
numbers. It was a very formal piece, in that it did not have a
narrative, but was strictly concerned with movement and patterns; nevertheless, it moved so fast and was so funny that it
became a particular favourite in the repertoire.

Field Study (1984)

Choreography: David Gordon. *Music:* John Field.
Lighting design: Mike Seignior.

The dancers also talked in this piece – non-stop through the first
section, and intermittently throughout the rest of the piece, dur-

12XU (1983) choreographed by Michael Clark for Extemporary Dance Theatre. Dancers: Yaakov Slivkin and Lloyd Newson. Photo: Dee Conway.

ing which sections from Field's piano music were played. As in *Counter Revolution*, the audience was meant to think of the dancers as real people, not just moving bodies. So in the opening section, the dancers not only talked, they also moved round a group of chairs, sitting and walking around them as if they were at a tea party. Then these everyday movements became closer to dance, as the dancers leaned against the chairs in arabesque or performed choreographed dance sequences with each other.

Dance then gave way to wilder activities. The dancers played hectic games of musical chairs, they raced across the stage, pulling chairs out from under each other, and they transformed the chairs into wheelbarrows or prams, carting each other around in them. Both pieces were typical of Gordon's method, which is to set himself a kind of technical task (for example, using numbers or chairs), and then to try and imagine all the different things he can make happen with it. His works can often end up being highly expressive (funny, cruel, tender) even though they do not tell a story.

95

From being a relatively successful, but increasingly mainstream company, Extemporary Dance Theatre became one of the most innovative and popular touring groups in Britain. The company did an enormous amount to familiarise audiences with new kinds of dance, not only through the diversity of its repertoire, but also through the work of its growing team of educationalists. In many of the towns where it performed this team led workshops in schools, arts centres and colleges, giving audiences both theoretical and practical insights into the works in the company's programme.

Successful as her policies were however, 1985 saw Claid ready to make more changes. She felt that it was impossible for one group of dancers, however skilled, to perform a really wide range of styles. Inevitably there were some members of the company who could adapt better to certain kinds of choreography than to others. So she decided to abandon the old system of keeping several works in the repertoire for two or three years, and of having one stable group of dancers. Instead she developed the idea, unique in this country, of having the company work on one project at a time – whether it was a single full-length piece or a programme of short works – and of choosing a specific group of dancers and musicians who would be most suited to it. After touring the project for a season, a new one would be planned and a new company selected. Certain dancers, even certain choreographers, might still be quite closely associated with the company, but essentially Extemporary Dance Theatre would live up to its name as a company with only a temporary structure and a commitment to continual change.

Important work (1985–87)

One of the major advantages of this policy was that it freed the company to work on a much larger and more elaborate scale. In 1986 for example, Claid choreographed a long piece, *Pierides*, in collaboration with jazz musicians Mike and Kate Westbrook. Because the company was performing the piece for one season only, the musicians could tour with the dancers, and be closely involved in the performance on stage. The other advantage was that it widened the scope of the repertoire even further, as in the programme of works by Laurie Booth and Steve Paxton, which demanded from its specially chosen dancers a

Counter Revolution (1981), choreographed by David Gordon, for Extemporary Dance Theatre. Photo: Dee Conway.

number of very particular skills in improvisation, contact and release work. The dancers for this project included Nigel Charnock, Michelle Richecoeur and Yolande Snaith, and the idea behind the programme was to introduce audiences to some of the principles behind the New Dance movement – the ideas that everyday movement can be as exciting and beautiful to watch as highly technical dancing, that dance doesn't have to tell a story or have beautiful designs, that dance can be improvised as well as completely set and polished.

Elbow Room (1986)
Choreography: Laurie Booth. *Design consultant:* Helen Turner.

This was made in accordance with certain rules, which were explained in the programme. In the first section Booth had devised a group of movements, very much in his own style, with which the dancers then improvised during performance. In the second section there were a series of choreographed 'elbow duets', in which the dancers tweaked, twisted and pulled at each other with a furious energy; and the third section was mostly created by the dancers, with movement based on the instruction of 'moving in one direction, but indicating the opposite at the same time'. Parts of this were set, parts were improvised.

Some of the dancing in this piece was pure Booth, with very ordinary gestures followed by explosive kicks, dives and corkscrew turns. But the piece also showed how difficult Booth's style is to perfect and how taxing the process of improvisation is on the performers. Several of the dancers were rather at a loss as to what to do (at least in the early performances) and few had Booth's clarity and boldness of gesture.

Audible Scenery (1986)
Choreography: Steve Paxton. *Design consultant:* Helen Turner.

For this piece, a low frill of curtains transformed the stage into a kind of boxing ring, while at three-minute intervals two musicians whistled a duet for half-time, allowing the dancers to warm up and chat like athletes. In between these pauses, the dancers performed a series of sporting movements – freezing in flying rugby tackles, or in tense hurdling strides, and going through the motions of catching, kicking and heading balls. At times these movements were woven into long, roundabout phrases of dance, and some of them were turned into jokes, like the moment when two dancers rushed to catch the same ball, and collided obsessively over and over again, or when individuals were caught in bored, cross or compromising positions.

The dancers had taken all these movements from sports photos. They were allowed to choose their own gestures and actions and to improvise the movements which linked them together. But in order to avoid chaos, there were fixed moments where they all had to be in certain places at certain times.

As in *Elbow Room*, however, some of the dancers were not always competent enough at improvising, and not always clear enough in their gestures to make these everyday actions interesting. Consequently the programme did not really succeed, as Claid had hoped, in making Booth and Paxton's work more accessible.

The last of these special projects was the all women show *Grace and Glitter* (1987). Made collaboratively by Claid, Maggie

Field Study (1984), choreographed by David Gordon for Extemporary Dance Theatre. The dancers here are Jon Smart, Lloyd Newson and Lindsey Butcher. Photo: Dee Conway.

Semple (a writer), and the six dancers, the piece explored issues concerning women's power and friendship through dance, speech and various props. For example, an energetic movement sequence of leaps and kicks showed off the women's strength and athleticism, while a contrasting scene explored the harassment to which women are exposed on the streets. At first the dancers cowered in positions of terror as the overamplifed screech of cars signalled the danger of rape, but then a sudden change of scale turned the whole situation upside down. Assuming positions of confidence and strength, the women looked down at a tiny model car that buzzed ineffectually at their feet, the male threat reduced to a little toy by their newfound power.

In 1988 Claid rethought Extemporary's set-up once again, and returned to the idea of evenings of mixed work. These involved

99

more collaboration – not only within the company but also between writers and choreographers. The company's repertoire for 1988 included a piece by Claid and the playwright Tasha Fairbanks, and an ariel ballet by Sue Broadway from the 'post-modern circus' Ra Ra Zoo. In 1990 Claid was replaced by a new artistic director, Sean Walsh, but the company disbanded in 1991 (see Conclusion).

Second Stride

Second Stride was formed in 1982 by three choreographers: Richard Alston, Siobhan Davies and Ian Spink. All three had had close contact with each other for several years – Davies and Alston had worked together since they were students at The Place; Spink had danced in works by both Davies and Alston; Davies had not only performed in Alston's choreography but had toured one of his works in her own company's programme.

Initially each choreographer had formed a separate company – Richard Alston and Dancers (1977–80), The Ian Spink Group (1978–81), and Siobhan Davies and Dancers (1981) – though several dancers actually performed with more than one group during this period.

Origins of Second Stride

Richard Alston and Dancers

When Richard Alston returned from America in 1977 he began making work both for London Contemporary Dance Theatre and for his own group, Richard Alston and Dancers. His best-known work from this period is *Doublework* (1978), and it was this piece that established him as a major choreographer, winning rave reviews from the critics. In 1980 Alston was invited to become Associate Choreographer with Ballet Rambert, and in 1986 he took over as Artistic Director.

Doublework (1978, revised 1982)
Choreography: Richard Alston. *Music (for 1982 revision):* James Fulkerson. *Costumes:* Jenny Henry.

This was a piece for three couples, all of whom had danced

Audible Scenery (1986) choreographed by Steven Paxton for Extemporary Dance Theatre. Dancers: Kathy Crick and Michelle Richecouer. Photo: Dee Conway.

together over a period of several years: Maedée Duprès and Julyen Hamilton, who had been with Rosemary Butcher; Michele Smith and Ian Spink, who had performed together in Australia; and Siobhan Davies and Alston himself, who had first danced together in 1968 in Alston's piece, *Transit*. (In the first performances Alston was actually replaced by Tom Jobe, due to injury.)

101

At first the piece was performed in silence, but in 1982 Alston revised and abridged it slightly, while at the same time adding a score for amplified string quartet by James Fulkerson. As its title suggests, the work's central idea was partnering. But another important aspect of its structure was the way that movements and phrases were repeated/doubled at different times, sometimes by different dancers, sometimes in different groupings and sometimes from different angles, so that the audience kept seeing the same material in different contexts. Alston also made strong use of contrast, with, for example a slow duet going on at the same time as a fast solo.

The opening duet (Duprès and Hamilton) was very soft and sustained, the dancers sinking their weight into each other or lifting each other, with neither man nor woman doing more of the work. It closed with a lift where Duprès wrapped her body around Hamilton's waist and was spun round and round in the air. Half way through their duet, another one began (Davies and Alston) which consisted of supported hinges and sinking lunges. Then, as the second couple left the stage, Michele Smith performed a solo, circling the stage with hops, *relevés* and turns, reckless lunges and a swinging torso – a light fast piece of dancing that emphasised her individuality against the other couple's togetherness. After this solo, the second couple returned, the four dancers performing parts of each other's duet.

In another duet between Duprès and Hamilton, there was a contrast between the initial 'contact element' (in which the dancers maintained constant physical connection) and the closing sequence, which was very fast and separate, a series of *relevés*, *bourrées*, *pirouettes* and *ronds de jambe*. This turned into a unison passage for four dancers with the entrance of Smith and Spink.

Traditionally, duets tend to dramatise the love (or hatred) between a man and a woman, but most of *Doublework* evoked no specific emotions, other than the kind of closeness and trust necessary for two dancers to work together. (The formal nature of the piece was emphasised by the plain practice clothes which the dancers wore.) But the final duet was more emotional. Although much of the movement was similar to what had gone before, it was performed in a more intimate way. Arms were clasped round the waist, not just as a means of support, but as a kind of clinging embrace. Davies wrapped her arms round Alston's neck and was carried in his arms like a sleeping child, and at the end

Doublework (1978, revised 1982). This shows the 1982 version for Second Stride, with Siobhan Davies, Richard Alston, Maedée Duprès and Julyen Hamilton. Photo: David Buckland.

he lowered her to the ground curving right over her in a gesture of intimacy and tenderness. (See Angela Kane's detailed description of this piece as it was recorded on video, *Dance Theatre Journal* 4:1, Spring 1986, pp. 8–9.)

The Ian Spink Group

Ian Spink trained at the Australian Ballet School and danced with The Australian Ballet between 1969 and 1974 and the Dance Company of New South Wales until 1978. Around 1974 he became interested in choreography and made various small-scale works. His work was first influenced by the spare economical style of Jaap Flier and later by Cunningham, with whose company he took class during an Australian tour. Two other Australians, Russell Dumas and Nanette Hassall, also introduced Spink to the work of American choreographers like Yvonne Rainer and Trisha Brown.

In 1978 Spink came to England to take part in the

Gulbenkian Summer Course for Professional Choreographers and Composers. Here he met several members of the X6 dance collective, including Tim Lamford with whom he made his first piece in London, *Low Budget Dances*. He was also very influenced by Mary Fulkerson's use of pedestrian movement and theatrical images, but even while absorbing these ideas, Spink took classes with Richard Alston, retaining his interest in pure dance technique.

In the same year he formed a small company, The Ian Spink Group, which included the dancers Michele Smith and Betsy Gregory. He also showed his first programme of work at X6 called 'Three Lesser-Known Works', which included *26 Solos* (1978). This work was important because it was made in collaboration with the designer Craig Givens, and featured the kind of close connection between movement and visual design that was to become so essential to his work.

In 1980 the Ian Spink Group took up a residency at the Roehampton Institute of Higher Education, the first of its kind in Britain, which lasted nearly a year. During this time, Spink made several works, including *De Gas* (1981).

De Gas was made in collaboration with the designer Antony McDonald and composer Jane Wells. It was based on Degas' paintings of women washing and drying themselves, but it was actually performed by three men. During the course of the piece they gradually removed their evening dress, washed their feet in enamel bowls and dried themselves on large bath towels. But these very ordinary movements were translated into phrases of dance by the graceful unison with which they were performed and by the careful grouping of the dancers on stage. A very typical moment was the passage when the three men simultaneously removed arm bands from their pockets and pushed them, with elegant finesse, onto their arms. They then adjusted their cuffs, repeated the whole procedure with the other arm, and turned away to perform the whole sequence facing another direction.

Spink's interest in repetition and variation (performing the same movements over and over again, but with slight changes and additions to the material) was not just confined to his treatment of ordinary movement: it was also a strong feature of his more 'danced' works like *Canta* (1981). The movement in this piece was influenced by Cunningham, contact and ballet, but it was also strongly affected by Spink's discovery of systems music,

Canta (1981), choreographed by Ian Spink for Second Stride. Dancers: Michael Clark, Betsy Gregory and Michele Smith. Photo: Chris Harris.

which uses repetition in a very mathematical way. Spink describes this as follows:

> . . . the repetition of bars and the use of [certain] devices, such as increasing or decreasing the number of counts in a bar, made me very aware of how those kind of ideas could be applied in choreography, for example through repeating steps, or decreasing them and increasing them systemically in the piece.

> (Interview with Sarah Rubidge in
> *Dance Theatre Journal* 5:2, 1987 p. 11)

In 1982 Spink created *Secret Garden* in which he worked with both actors and dancers. It was a piece using both speech and movement and it developed out of long periods of improvisation in which the performers explored their own lives and feelings to create material for the work. This new method of working was one which Spink was to develop more fully in his choreography with Second Stride.

Siobhan Davies and Dancers

Unlike most of the other choreographers discussed in this book, Davies spent much of her early career as a dancer and a choreographer with an established company – London Contemporary Dance Theatre. But she was also interested in working in a smaller, more experimental environment and in 1981 she took a sabbatical in order to set up her own company. Like Alston her work was strongly influenced by Cunningham, though her movements had a distinctive fluidity and weight.

Among her company were Paul Claydon, Duprès, Mary Evelyn, Juliet Fisher and Jonathan Lunn, and the first programme consisted of *Standing Waves* (1981) to a piece of improvised trombone music by Stuart Dempster, and the gravely beautiful *Plain Song* (1981) to music by Erik Satie. Also in the programme was a piece by Alston, *The Field of Mustard* (1980), a duet for Davies and Fisher. Both *Plainsong* and *The Field of Mustard* were taken into the Second Stride repertoire. After leaving both Second Stride and London Contemporary Dance Theatre, Davies set up her own company again in 1988 (see Conclusion).

Second Stride

The company's name was chosen with an obvious reference to Alston's first group, Strider, and it was initially formed to last only one season. The three choreographers saw it as a convenient way of presenting their work together and pooling their dancers, even though there were a number of obvious differences between their various styles. Spink's interest was in strict repetitive movement and experimental theatre; Davies' style tended to be much softer and more straightforwardly concerned with character and relationships, and Alston's choreography focused on fast, rhythmic footwork and precisely placed positions.

Yet there were also similarities. All three had been influenced by Cunningham, ballet, and by contact and release, and all three created movement that was very pure and uncluttered, and which rarely indulged in grand pyrotechnics like big leaps or dramatic falls. Even where the choreography might express emo-

---

SIOBHAN DAVIES AND DANCERS
Theatre Royal, Stratford East - Sunday 1st March, 1981

STANDING WAVES (1981)

Choreography: Siobhan Davies*
Music: Standing Waves 1976, by Stuart Dempster,
                    improvising on the trombone in the Great
                    Abbey of Pope Clement VI, Avignon
Design: David Buckland*
Lighting: Peter Mumford*
Dancers: Paul Clayden, Siobhan Davies, Maedée Duprès,
                    Mary Evelyn, Juliet Fisher, Jonathan Lunn,
                    Jeremy Nelson

PAUSE

THE FIELD OF MUSTARD (1980)
for Robin Howard

Choreography: Richard Alston
Music: Six Studies in English Folk Song for cello
                    and piano by Ralph Vaughan Williams
                    (by kind permission of Stainer and Bell)
Lighting: Peter Mumford*
Dancers: Siobhan Davies, Juliet Fisher

This dance is based on images remembered from reading the
'Field of Mustard', a short story by A.E.Coppard.

INTERVAL

PLAIN SONG (1981)

Choreography: Siobhan Davies*
Music: Erik Satie
                    Two Préludes (1893): Fête Donnée par des
                    Chevaliers Normands en l'Honneur d'une
                    Jeune Demoiselle; D'Eginhard
                    Ogives (1886) (by kind permission of
                                    Chant du Monde/UMP)
                    Messe des Pauvres (1895)
Piano: Michael Finnissy
Design: David Buckland*
Lighting: Peter Mumford*
Dancers: Paul Clayden, Siobhan Davies, Maedée Duprès,
                    Mary Evelyn, Juliet Fisher, Jonathan Lunn,
                    Jeremy Nelson

Programme for Siobhan Davies and Dancers, 1981.

tion, it never did so in a dramatic or obvious way – there was always a sense of understatement that contrasted with the more emotive works of companies like London Contemporary Dance Theatre.

In addition to these shared qualities, all three choreographers

107

were interested in working with artists from other disciplines, commissioning new music and working closely with visual artists so that dance, music and design began from the same starting point. The dancers in the company were experienced, and often highly individual performers, able to deal with the demanding movement of Alston's work as well as the acting skills demanded by Spink's. Some of them were originally members of larger companies like London Contemporary Dance Theatre and Ballet Rambert, who had left because they wanted to perform more varied work.

Second Stride's first programme was toured throughout Britain and America and was very well reviewed. It included Alston's *Doublework* and *The Field of Mustard*, Davies's *Rushes*, *Plainsong* and *Carnival*, and Spink's *There is No Other Woman*, *Canta* and *De Gas*. After producing another new work for the company's second season (*Java*), Alston's commitments with Ballet Rambert forced him to withdraw, but Spink and Davies continued to keep Second Stride afloat for limited seasons each year.

Initially, Davies and Spink each produced half of a double-bill, though they later took on alternate programmes, and when Davies's commitments kept her apart from the company during 1986 and 1987, the repertoire was exclusively by Spink.

In 1988 Second Stride was invited to become the resident dance company at the new Towngate Theatre in Basildon. In the same year Davies launched her own new company.

Important work

Carnival (1982)
Choreography: Siobhan Davies. *Music:* Camille Saint-Saëns. *Design:* Antony McDonald.

Set to Saint-Saëns' *Carnival of the Animals*, this had a backdrop of a jungle, painted Rousseau-style, in which tigers lurked alongside the face of the composer. The choreography was created for twelve dancers, and it came in the form of brief vignettes, each one showing a different animal or pair of animals. Philippe Giraudeau, for instance, danced the dying swan solo (a witty gender reversal of the great female role danced by Anna Pavlova). Ingenious passages of mime indicated the swan's

Plain Song (1981), choreographed by Siobhan Davies, performed here by Second Stride. Photo: David Buckland.

appearance – a raised hand made the shape of a swan's neck, while a forward crouch, with the hands joined together behind the back, looked like a swan plunging into the water. The choreography was a mix of awkwardness and grace, and Giraudeau performed it with a dignified slowness that emphasised the character's loneliness.

Spink and Davies appeared as a couple of 'Darby and Joan' tortoises – doubled over, clutching each other for security, and

109

staring around in short-sighted panic. There were also a couple of lolling lions, a love-lorn cuckoo and a bounding wild ass, and throughout the piece Davies managed to intrigue her audience not only with the comic/pathetic mannerisms of the animals but also with the inventiveness of the movement.

Silent Partners (1984)
Choreography: Siobhan Davies. *Design:* David Buckland.

This piece also had a narrative of a kind, portraying a couple's relationship through the friendships and love affairs which they had had prior to meeting. The dance was constructed almost entirely out of duets, which communicated the quality of the relationships without any mime or acting.

For example, the dancers' feelings could be seen from the way they held or lifted each other, and by the quality (nervous, trusting or ecstatic) of their movements. The effect that each relationship had on the two lovers (Michele Smith and Philippe Giraudeau) was shown by the movements which each picked up from their previous partners. These new movements became part of the lover's own style, like ideas and influences which they had absorbed. The partners from these early duets also gathered in the background, behind a transparent screen, as if they were still hovering in Smith's and Giraudeau's memories.

The piece opened with a duet between Maedée Duprès and Ikky Maas, which was a kind of prologue, conveying the idea of people simply dancing, as in a dance hall. Then Smith entered to dance with Juliet Fisher, a slow quiet duet in which Fisher seemed to instruct and dominate Smith – almost like a mother figure. After that Smith danced with Michael Popper who made her adapt to a completely different set of movements.

The third duet was between Giraudeau and Lenny Westerdijk and they danced as if they had known each other for a long time, touching each other and balancing against each other as if they were very dependent. In complete contrast, Giraudeau then danced with Cathy Burge, each performing very different movements and hardly making any kind of contact at all. The next duet was between Smith and Duprès, the latter teaching Smith a more sensuous kind of movement while Giraudeau and Maas also danced together. Finally Smith and Giraudeau joined for their own duet.

In this concluding section, movements from the other duets were echoed, while the dancers explored their new relationship, using much larger movements of the body that suggested the passion and commitment of their feelings. The dancers were dressed in simple evening clothes, suggesting the appearance of ordinary people rather than dancers.

New Tactics (1983)
Choreography: Ian Spink. *Music:* Orlando Gough.
Design: Antony McDonald, Craig Givens.

This was an important work for Spink because it involved collaboration with so many people. The dancers were involved in creating the material via movement improvisation and games of word association; and writer Tim Albery, composer Orlando Gough and designer Antony McDonald contributed their ideas at every stage.

The piece used dance, speech and props to examine the way people think and feel when they are poised between dreaming and waking. All of the dancers revealed distinct characters through their movement and speech – the 'eccentric self-assertiveness of Sally Owen, the loping . . . vulnerability of Davies, the romantic cool of Giraudeau' (see Alastair Macaulay's review in *Dance Theatre Journal* 1983, 1:4 pp. 8–12).

In one scene they mimed or talked through the process of settling down to sleep, and the stage was covered in pillows and duvets. Juliet Fisher said, 'Was there anything special about today, yes that moment . . . I'll write that down . . . some time', and Giraudeau counted sheep. When sleep failed to come, the dancers recycled the actions of the day, performing everyday movements like wiping faces and running fingers through their hair, but in such a rhythmic way that the movements became stylised, and developed into simple dance phrases. Finally everyone went to sleep.

Further and Further into Night (1984)
Choreography: Ian Spink. *Music:* Orlando Gough.
Design: Antony McDonald.

This was based on Alfred Hitchcock's film *Notorious*, with the dancers wearing elegant forties clothes similar to those worn in

111

the film. Spink took gestures and words from certain scenes and then, as in *De Gas*, repeated them with different variations. The tying of a scarf round the waist or drinking out of a glass would be performed by the dancers in unison or in canon, and the performers were always arranged in neat formal groupings around the stage. Orlando Gough's repetitive score emphasised the way the dancers repeated the same words and actions over and over again.

Because of this very formalised treatment, little was left of the original story, although the designs remained faithful to the style of the film, with walls and doors in black formica, and dramatic, Hitchcockian lighting that fell in shafts across the floor. But the piece took on its own distinctive drama when different fragments of action were played out by different dancers, particularly when men's parts were played by women and vice versa. A woman pleading to a man became two women pleading to one man, became one man pleading to two women – all three variations having very different emotional and sexual implications. On the surface, the piece was so formal, so cool, that the violence of certain gestures was exaggerated and the piece became a study of the aggression that lies beneath the surface of social conventions.

Bösendorfer Waltzes (1986)
Choreography: Ian Spink. *Music:* Orlando Gough.
Design: Antony McDonald.

Spink says of this piece:

> . . . we were trying to create a situation whereby one could look at the piece as if it was a dream where things don't necessarily connect – or where they connect on a deeper level, more on a subconscious level. We used everything that was on hand – words, ideas, pictures, movement and music. We tried to be as free as possible, moving between these different things. It was very difficult for the audience to just see and then understand.
>
> (Interview with Sarah Rubidge,
> *Dance Theatre Journal* 1987, 5:2, p. 12)

The raw material which inspired this piece was a combination of

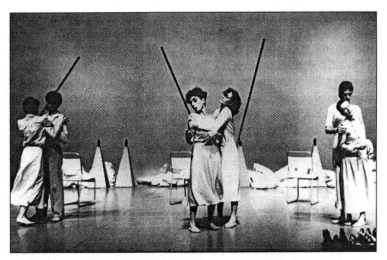

New Tactics (1983), choreographed by Ian Spink and Tim Albery for Second Stride. Photo: Chris Harris.

Fokine's ballet *The Firebird*, and the Surrealist movement in painting and poetry which hit Europe during the 1920s and 1930s. The end product was considered by some as inspired chaos, by others as downright nonsense.

The work began with speeches that were devised and spoken by the six dancers in which they talked about themselves as if to a psychiatrist (i.e. in a stream of often disconnected thoughts and images). The stage was littered with an incongruous array of props – including blackboards, miniature houses and a psychiatrist's couch on which Cathy Burge lay, while Philippe Giraudeau broke an egg into a bowl that rested on her back.

Throughout the piece the dancers told stories, danced sections of Spink's characteristically clear and repetitive choreography, and dismantled the houses to uncover four grand pianos (the Bösendorfers of the title) on which the dancers and musicians played. Objects symbolised different things, so that, for instance, the psychiatrist's couch was also used as a dining table and a gynaecologist's couch. Even though the dancers' speeches sometimes made obvious historical reference to figures associated with the Surrealist movement, the audience was often left to make whatever they chose, or didn't choose, of the content.

Other sections of the piece were based on *The Firebird*, which

113

Spink had reworked to bring out a new level of aggression in the story. The role of the Firebird was played by both Sally Owen and Cathy Burge, and they struggled viciously with the Prince (Giraudeau) who was trying to capture them. This fight added new implications to the simple Russian tale. For instance there was something almost masochistic in the way that the exhausted Owen kept coming back for more physical punishment; and the way that Giraudeau moved from brutality to almost gentle concern suggested that they were lovers who knew each other very well and had been having the same argument for years.

The scene where Fokine shows twelve princesses playing catch with golden apples was also given a much more aggressive slant, with the dancers hurling real apples all over the stage, and splattering them against the wall with a violence that was totally unlike the decorousness of the original. On a similarly bizarre note, the wicked magician Kastchei was defeated, not by the dramatic destruction of a huge magic egg, but by Giraudeau breaking an ordinary chicken's egg over Ikky Maas's head.

As in *Further and Further into Night* the dancers often doubled up as the same character, or swapped parts, and there was a similar reversal of sex roles. At one point Giraudeau, dressed as a dapper little matador, was paraded in arabesque by another man, very much as if he had been put on display for the woman who was watching him. The piece ended with Sally Owen making an impassioned speech about the sacredness of the artist's freedom; the work's attempt to mix so many art forms and ideas could itself be seen as a statement of its own liberation from convention.

Audiences were very divided about *Bösendorfer Waltzes* – some enjoying the richness and strangeness of the material, others complaining that they couldn't make head or tail of it. (It certainly helped if you knew *The Firebird* and had some background information on the Surrealists.)

Weighing the Heart (1987)
Choreography: Ian Spink. *Music:* Orlando Gough and Man Jumping. *Design:* Antony McDonald.

The inspiration for this piece was religious myth and ritual, and the work brought together stories from Ancient Egyptian myth, from The Bible, from *The Magic Flute* and many other sources.

Further and Further into Night (1984), choreographed by Ian Spink for Second Stride. Dancers: Juliet Fisher, Michele Smith. Photo: Chris Harris.

Again there was nothing resembling a straightforward narrative. Yet the fragmented plots were presented in an almost comic-strip fashion; there were sections of pure dance where you didn't

115

have to worry too much about the meaning, and the music kept the whole thing moving at a fast and entertaining pace. There were also extensive programme notes to satisfy those who wanted to know what each scene was all about.

Michael Clark

Michael Clark took ballet and Scottish dance classes from an early age in Aberdeen and then studied at The Royal Ballet School. His unusual gifts were quickly recognised, but Clark found the atmosphere of the school stifling. He felt that it was not only out of touch with the real world, but that it seemed isolated from the rest of dance. 'The training you get there is really blinkered,' he has said, 'people aren't interested in modern dance; they think that modern dancers are just ballet dancers who can't jump' (interview with author, 1987).

At seventeen he left the school to join Ballet Rambert, where he appeared in several works by Richard Alston. In 1981 he left Rambert to work with other choreographers (including Ian Spink) and in the same year attended the International Summer School for Choreographers and Composers which was led by Merce Cunningham. (Cunningham's style, via Richard Alston and Karole Armitage, was to have an important influence on Clark's own work.)

He also appeared in Armitage's *Drastic Classicism* (1982) and created his first important piece, *Of a Feather Flock* (1982), for her and five other dancers including himself. The next year Riverside Studios appointed him as choreographer-in-residence, and during the following eighteen months Clark made a large number of works not only for himself but for Extemporary Dance Theatre, Mantis Dance Company and English Dance Theatre. By 1984 he began to work regularly with Ellen van Schuylenburch, for example on the duet version of *New Puritans*, and in the summer of 1984 they expanded to become Michael Clark and Company with a succession of other dancers, including Matthew Hawkins, Leslie Bryant and Julie Hood.

Clark's company has toured throughout Britain and the world, and has appeared on British and American television. Much of its repertoire has been made in close collaboration with the film-maker Charles Atlas, designers Leigh Bowery and

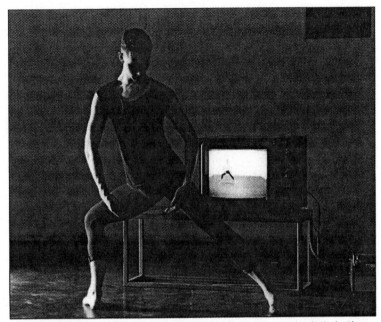

Parts I–IV (1983) choreographed by Michael Clark. Dancer: Michael Clark. Photo: Dee Conway.

BodyMap, and the Manchester rock band The Fall. During its early years the company received funds from GLAA and the Arts Council though it later became one of the few independent dance groups to make a reasonable commercial success.

Clark's work has been through various stages, all of which show his desire to break away from his ballet training and the values of what he sees as the establishment. At the beginning he chose to work with untrained (or very differently trained) dancers as a way of distancing himself from his own classical background.

Important work

Parts I–IV (1983)
Choreography: Michael Clark. *Music:* Glenn Branca, Hugh Griffiths, Robert Rental, John Marc Gowans, Mark Rowlatt.

The following description is taken from Chris Savage-King's

review in *Dance Theatre Journal* (1983, 1:4 pp. 30–32) and shows the mixture of movement styles which Clark was exploring:

> Part I opens with a child performing some classical highland dancing. The . . . music begins to slur and one by one the others join in with a cool, silky adagio . . . Gaby Agis and Michael Clark . . . are in a duet, she all strong and tense, he wispy and buoyant. She supports him in arabesque, he leans on her and the traditional pas de deux is inverted. Gregory Nash . . . offers a neurotic interlude of jabbed shoulders and knees . . . with razor sharp turns. Ikky Maas enters and pulls him across his body into an attitude inside out; his head lolls.
>
> Steve Goff and Gaby Agis walk past each other . . . Her gaze remains on him and suddenly there is a chase. She's still aggressive, pulling punches over his head while Goff imitates Nash's twitches . . .
>
> In Part II a colour card is shown on the video at the back . . . After a . . . closely-woven trio for three men, they fetch Agis from the side. She's hauled in like an aeroplane and wearing black leather gloves . . . The video is brought down stage. Its lights – the only light now – shine on Goff and Cathrine Price as they are tied with a rope by Agis. Clark flickers around them, then darts off, returning to turn off the video . . . the mood throughout has been . . . very 1980s . . . troubled and aggressive.
>
> In Part III three videos are at the front; they show Clark, then the others, in various stages of motion at slightly staggered times, from different angles. The music . . . is a mixture of gurgles, feedback and the sort of noise wild animals would make if run by computers. It grates abominably on the inner ear. Clark appears now and then to repeat and elaborate the moves shown by the videos. Meanwhile a technician is laboriously moving the machine backwards. (Clark performs a solo) then is dragged off by the technician . . .
>
> The music grows dangerous. For the last section it's Indian twangs, African drums and rock guitars. Clark is wearing a floppy tutu and a ripped T-shirt whose long sleeves cover his hands . . . His backside wriggles and he embraces himself with his arms: it's narcissistic, a touch coy. There's a last burst of energy – *chaînés*, a leap or two, then he's off.

Parts I–IV contained certain elements that were to be repeated in Clark's later work: the jumble of different events with no clear theme or structure linking them together; the sometimes painfully loud rock music mixed with other musical styles; the mixing of pure dance with everyday gestures, mime and visual jokes; the highlighting of the production's mechanics (like the technician appearing on stage) and above all the use of outrageous costumes and gestures which reverse sexual roles (Clark dressed up as a coy ballerina).

When Clark started collaborating with designers Leigh Bowery and BodyMap, many of these aspects became more extreme and his work was more obviously made to shock and provoke, as well as to appeal to a young, fashion-conscious public.

New Puritans (1984)
Choreography: Michael Clark. *Music:* The Fall.
Costumes: Leigh Bowery. *Lighting:* Charles Atlas.

In the original duet form of the piece (which was later revised for four dancers) Clark and Ellen van Schuylenburch wore outsize platform shoes, bizarre make-up and romper suits which revealed their bare buttocks. Much of the piece was pure dance (the platform soles acting as clumpy versions of pointe shoes) and Clark and Schuylenburch raced through bravura turns, high slashing kicks and tricksy partnering.

But elements of it were also very disturbing, like Clark's adoption of a female persona, first demure and then lascivious, and the blatant aggression of some of his gestures – spitting on the floor making 'up yours' signs, and swallowing a live goldfish.

In later works there were similar acts of deliberate 'bad taste'. In *our caca phoney H. our caca phoney H.* (1985) – a spoof on the musical *Hair* and sixties pop culture – the women were dressed in very butch outfits while the men were coy and camp in female dress. As in many other works there was a lot of explicit 'sexual' material. *Pure Pre-Scenes* (1987) contained a tape of a woman masturbating, and *Because We Must* (1987) had a nude final scene. Certain feminists have found these images offensive, because they feel that although Clark might be challenging

119

accepted sexual norms, he does so by ridiculing women, but not men.

As well as including provocative sexual images, Clark began to cast friends, like Leigh Bowery and David Nolah from BodyMap, in his pieces. This was partly to underline the connection between his work and his personal life, since so much of his choreography has been rooted in the way he lives – the clothes he wears, the jokes he enjoys, the music he listens to and the subjects that are important to him, like gay rights. Often the point has been obscured however, because many of Bowery's and Nolah's contributions have ended up as childish jokes that have irritated as many people as they have amused. In *Pure Pre-Scenes* Bowery watered a prostrate pianist with a giant 'penis', while Nolah busied around on stage cooking a meal.

Another disturbing feature of Clark's work has been the inclusion of fascist-style behaviour – goose-stepping, Nazi salutes, and the band Liebach who chanted Hitler's speeches throughout the third act of *No Fire Escape in Hell* (1986).

Many people have felt that Clark has used all this provocative material simply to cause a 'frisson' of scandal. Certainly he admits that at the beginning he was motivated by a desire to shock, to go against all the polite assumptions of the ballet world in which he was brought up. He also argues that he wanted 'to bring in a new audience for dance', that he didn't want to make work 'that was just for other dancers and choreographers and critics' and that he had lost faith in what could be said with pure movement.

In fact Clark has been very successful in winning a new audience for his work, having a sell-out season at Sadler's Wells Theatre for *No Fire Escape*, and another success with *Because We Must*. There were many people at these performances who were not dance-lovers, but who were responding to something that was very close to their own culture – the music, the fancy dress, the explicit gestures and the sometimes obscure humour.

Despite the fast-moving, often frivolous nature of Clark's work, he also claims that it is meant to make people think seriously. He doesn't present a simple message, but argues that when, for instance, he used the masturbation tape to accompany a lyrical female trio, he wanted people to question the two contrasting images of women. And he says that he has used fascist

Our caca phoney H. our caca phoney H. (1985) choreographed by Michael Clark. Dancer: Michael Clark. Photo: Dee Conway.

images in his work as a way of 'testing people's responses' or of trying to make them uncomfortable.

Some critics would argue that Clark's work doesn't have a clear enough point of view for these elements to make a serious political impact. Yet few argue with Clark's talent for making beautiful and exciting movement. All of his works have contained inventive and fluent passages of dance and the work that he made for Ballet Rambert, *Swamp*, showed that he was capable of making a piece of sustained dance without any other elements.

Swamp (1986)
Choreography: Michael Clark. *Music:* Bruce Gilbert.
Design: BodyMap. *Lighting and projections:* Charles Atlas.

This piece was a development from an earlier work *Do You Me? I Did* which Clark had made on his own company in 1984. Its inspiration came from the film of Edward Albee's play, *Who's Afraid of Virginia Woolf?* (in which Elizabeth Taylor addresses Richard Burton as 'hey swampy'). In *Swamp*'s early performances, images from the film, and phrases from the dialogue spilled onto the back wall. But these were later abandoned, leaving the stage clear for the dancing. This started out as a series of duets which recreated the menacing, troubled relationships between the characters in the play. A nerve-screamingly slow adagio for a man and a woman contrasted with a punchily aggressive duet for another couple, which was full of high fighting kicks and electric flickerings of energy. Gradually all the dancers in the piece started banding together, at first in slow motion rolls and then in a tight almost militaristic formation. In a strict line, they marched across the stage, their arms slicing through the air in unison gestures. The piece closed as all the dancers dropped to the floor, leaving the main male dancer to dominate the stage in a long low arabesque.

In *Swamp* the excitement was not created through bizarre or shocking props, but through the pacing of the work – the build-up of energy and the contrast of slow movement against fast, and of large group sections against solos and duets.

Clark has recently said that he is now 'more confident that you can say a lot with pure dance' and he feels that 'other people have taken over the proppy, costumey side of things.' The second act of *Because We Must*, for example, was nearly all pure dance, though in true Clark form it ended with a loud rock section in which naked women played guitars.

DV8

While Michael Clark has challenged his audience by integrating provocative, even ugly gestures into virtuoso dance, the company DV8 has often used movement which is outside any traditional dance vocabulary. They have tended to avoid pointed feet, complex steps, high extensions, graceful arms, difficult jumps and so on, and many of their actions have looked brutal, violent and provocative.

DV8 was formed in 1986 by Lloyd Newson, who danced for several years with Extemporary Dance Theatre. Despite Claid's policy to explore different styles of dance and to present work that was relevant to a young audience, Newson felt the company's repertoire was not political or challenging enough. The two works he made for Extemporary showed the direction in which his own ideas were going: *Breaking Images* (1982) was an attack on the stereotyped sexual roles of dancers (and ordinary people) and *Beauty, Art and the Kitchen Sink* (1984) challenged the unreal image of perfection presented by mainstream modern dance and its distance from the complexities and conflicts of everyday life. The piece began with a sequence of pure, very technical dance, but gradually disintegrated as the woman soloist began to lose confidence, smearing her make-up, performing increasingly uncontrolled movements and finally destroying the set.

Newson felt that being in an established company limited his choreographic ideas – he couldn't always make the work he wanted and he disliked the fact that he was rarely allowed to contribute to works choreographed by other people.

So in 1985 he left Extemporary Dance Theatre to work freelance, and then in 1986 formed DV8. This company, he said, was about 'taking risks . . . about breaking down barriers, whether in dance, theatre or personal politics. It is about communicating ideas and feelings directly clearly and unpretentiously' (DV8 publicity, 1987). It was also a group where the dancers created the work in close collaboration with each other.

One of the first pieces which the company performed was a collaboration between Newson and Nigel Charnock called *My Sex Our Dance* (1986). This explored a male relationship, depicting raw emotions like violence, sexuality and aggression in very raw physical terms (the company believe that to reveal human feelings they often have to use very extreme movement). It began with the two men tensely clasping hands, then a furious tussle of wills developed, with Newson careering round the stage twisting and crashing to the floor while a gasping Charnock raced round after him trying to break his falls. As well as showing aggression they also showed tenderness and desire, making a truce with an embrace which virtually glued their bodies to each other.

Important work

Deep End (1987)
Choreography: Lloyd Newson. *Singer:* Paul Jones.
Lighting: Tina MacHugh.

This was a piece about relationships between men and women. But rather than presenting the happy-ever-after images of popular romance, it explored the power struggles that go on between the sexes. Newson and Charnock were joined by Michelle Richecoeur and Liz Ranken. Ranken, for example, dramatised the terrible masochism of a woman trying to attract an indifferent man – repeatedly hurling herself to the floor in an effort to get his attention. At the same time Newson and Richecoeur performed a simple dance duet, at first with him lifting her but then reversing the convention so that she became more powerful and took the initiative. Parts of the piece were very violent, and parts very funny, like Ranken's imitation of a women dancer trying to please her male judges. After testing out a few ballet moves, none of which worked successfully, she suddenly screamed, then paused, twiddled her hair with embarrassment and whispered, 'Is there anything else you would like me to do?'.

In *My Body Your Body* (1987) the company was joined by twelve other dancers. Based on Robin Norwood's book *Women Who Love Too Much*, it explored the ways in which women bind themselves to men, the way they try to seduce them, and to abase themselves. In the first section the eight women waited for

124

Deep End (1987), choreographed by DV8. Dancers: Liz Ranken and Michelle Richecoeur.

an agonisingly long time for their lovers, who never showed up. Then, when eight men finally appeared, the women set out to pursue them, chasing them up and down the stage, hobbled by their high heels and tight dresses. The women's desperate chase kept sending them sprawling onto the floor but even when they had finally caught hold of the men, they were simply thrown contemptuously aside.

125

Half-way through, the roles were reversed, and the men became subservient to the women. During an early section the women had lined up in pouting Playboy poses, but the men were now forced to do the same, teetering on high heels, showing themselves off in a degrading way. At the same time the women stormed through the audience cracking brutally obscene jokes. But at the end they were left in a calm, almost ambiguous mood, some of the women still hankering after their men, others absorbed in their own independent lives.

The Cholmondeleys

The Cholmondeleys is an all-women group, formed in 1984 by two Laban graduates, Lea Anderson and Teresa Barker.

Important work

The Cholmondeley Sisters (1984)
Choreography: Lea Anderson. *Music:* Drostan Madden.
Design: Jerome Parsons.

In this, their first and title piece, Anderson and Barker were dressed up in rustling frocks like haughty ballerinas, and went through a series of almost clichéd ballet steps – *pas de bourrées*, graceful poses and elaborate *ports de bras*. But at the same time they seemed to be distracted by other, more important preoccupations, sharing sweets with each other, checking their lipstick and searching for missing hairpins. The backing vocals were simply a list of objects such as sewing machines, sellotape and elastic bands, which sounded like a stream of humdrum thoughts running through the dancers' heads, completely unrelated to the dance or to the public image they were trying to present.

The Clichés and the Holidays (1985)
Choreography: Lea Anderson. *Music:* Traditional Catalan and Mexican street band. *Design:* Sandy Powell.

Such subversion of the dancer's image was also a strong element

DV8 physical theatre

LLOYD NEWSON

- founder member of DV8, has established himself as one of the leading performers and choreographers in the modern dance world. His controversial work, combining precision with raw theatricality, has attracted a wide range of critical opinion:

"A dancer of tremendous strength and versatility" Sunday Times

"...highly individual and splendid artist" The Guardian

"Insufferable" The Guardian

"Funny, punchy, the audience loved it..."

- Lloyd now joins forces with two exciting performers who bring to the company a strong determination to change the state of contemporary dance, which they see as stale, unimaginative and safe.

DV8 physical theatre

ARE YOU TIRED OF CONTEMPORARY DANCE?

DV8 is an independent collective of performers who have choreographed and danced with major dance companies in Britain, New Zealand and Australia. All have become disillusioned and frustrated with the current state of dance.

WHY?

1. Artistic output compromised to please funding bodies and to gain box-office returns.

2. Conservative and uninspiring choreography, producing similar dancers.

3. The concept of dance restricted to a set vocabulary of movement and concerns.

4. Continually reinforcing accepted values and traditions.

DV8 aims to break down these barriers. All the members share a similar political and personal commitment, and want to express this in their work. In doing so they hope to challenge the traditional values set up by the more established companies.

DV8's manifesto.

in this piece. It was choreographed for three dancers (including Gaynor Coward) and parodied the kind of Spanish dancing that is put on for tourists. The dancers wore flounced skirts with matador trousers underneath, so that they could take both male and female roles, and the movement was a mixture of bullfighting manoeuvres, tango, flamenco and peasant dance. Every cliché of Spanish dance was used, the high flamenco arches, the smouldering glances, the rustling skirts, the macho matador lunges and the mournful peasant dance. The dancers performed it with a tired and dutiful manner, often appearing to forget the audience, for example when the 'matador' lost 'himself' in loving contemplation of his own muscles, or another dancer checked to see if a button was missing. Sometimes they even got carried away, departing from the 'set' choreography to perform their own idiosyncratic gestures – a hand raised to play a castanet suddenly got involved in an elaborate flourish or a dancer paused in a backwards roll to do a little dance with her feet.

Dragon (1985)
Choreography: Lea Anderson. *Music:* Drostan Madden.
Costumes: Brand Spanking.

This very popular piece was not at all comic. The choreography had a furious energy, transforming the dancers into the kind of giant dragon puppets that tower over Chinese processions. In the first section the movement was performed as a solo, by Anderson, her arms miming angry slicing jaws, her legs thrusting out at odd reptilian angles and her set, ferocious glare giving her dancing a completely inhuman quality. The whole thing was then repeated as a duo and then as a trio, so that the power of the movement built up each time round.

In 1987 the group became a quartet (with Rossana Sen) and they started to create longer works, like *Marina*. There was a quirky, fishy quality about this choreography which was emphasised by the way the dancers' jackets were cut into seaweedy fronds. The music, by Bizet, Verdi and Rossini, gave a grave formality to the piece, as did the simple floor patterns and elementary ballet steps. But what often looked like a courtly dance was punctuated by arm movements that dived and

The Big Dance Number (1987), choreographed by Lea Anderson of The Cholmondeleys. The dancers here are Gaynor Coward and Lea Anderson. Photo: Chris Nash.

wriggled, hands that flapped and bodies that undulated with an occasional fishy flourish.

The Big Dance Number (1987)

Choreography: Lea Anderson. *Music:* Drostan Madden, Steve Blake, Jerome Kern. *Costumes:* Pam Downe.

This opened with the saccharine strains of an old Hollywood dance tune but the dancers did not wear ballgowns or dance waltzes: they were dressed in brown smocks and their movements were very constricted. Rooted to the spot, they arched and rippled their backs, weaving lavish and complicated shapes with their arms. Gradually though, the dance built up in complexity. Live musicians performed a strident atonal version of 'Just the Way You Look Tonight' and while Barker and Sen carried on doing very minimal movements the others started to dance a pastiche of Fred Astaire and Ginger Rogers. They circled the stage with fast, rhythmic steps and they ended by jumping over Sen and Barker, who were lying on the floor. This was a reference to one of Astaire's and Roger's most famous dances, which ends with them appearing to jump out of a window.

Yolande Snaith

Another important dancer and choreographer to appear in the 1980s was Dartington-trained Yolande Snaith. There are elements in Snaith's style which are similar to Booth's, such as her acrobatic dives and jumps, and the way she tips and balances her weight through a continuous stream of movement. Like Booth she often performs on her own, though she has collaborated with other dancers and film-makers. But what is most distinctive about her work is the way she uses props, costumes and lighting, to create strong visual images. Sometimes these images are presented for their own visual interest, but more often they show different facets of women. In one piece Snaith stood on a pedestal, draped in white cloth like a perfect, alabaster figurine; in another she was dressed in a satin corset, dragging around a wardrobe on which another women reclined, dressed in virginal white satin.

Important work

Scared Shirtless (1987)
Choreography: Yolande Snaith.

Here the choreography centred around one extraordinary prop – an oversized white shirt. It began with Snaith wearing this, and a broad-brimmed hat, advancing backwards with her arms stretched out like an ecclesiastic giving benediction. Then she turned round and sat down, edging backwards so that the full length of material billowed out across the floor. Finally she slipped out of the shirt completely, like a butterfly coming out of a cocoon. As she reached out for an apple hanging at her side, the strains of 'When a Man Loves a Woman' could be heard, and the lights went out.

Scared Shirtless (1987), choreographed and performed by Yolande Snaith. Photo: Chris Nash.

For the rest of the piece the shirt was hanging from a giant coat hanger, representing a looming male presence. At one point, Snaith wrapped herself in its sleeves, accompanied by a crooning love song ('Between these Arms'); at another, she arranged it over a chair and sat on its knees, darning one of its

131

sleeves, and at another she waltzed with it, flying around the stage until it twisted into a giant corkscrew.

Some of the ideas for this piece came from Gabriel Garcia Marquez's hallucinatory novel *One Hundred Years of Solitude*, such as the two yellow butterflies which Snaith wore over her eyes (referring to the character who sees butterflies every time her lover appears). In a general way, the piece seemed to reflect Marquez's portrayal of women as creatures locked away in their own private world. In her concluding solo Snaith started out as an old woman, brushing crumbs off her skirt, rocking a baby, and fanning herself; then she became a young girl dancing with a wild burst of energy before getting locked into the mechanical gestures of a trapped middle-aged wife.

Into the 90s

Since the previous chapters were completed, the landscape of the dance world has changed considerably. Certain companies have come into the foreground, others have become less visible, some unfortunately have folded. New trends, new attitudes have also crystallised. But before considering these, and considering what the term 'New Dance' now stands for, I should briefly update the histories of some of the companies mentioned.

As public funds get tighter, and the competition for Arts Council grants gets more intense, some companies have simply failed to survive. Extemporary Dance Theatre, after acquiring a new artistic director in Sean Walsh and giving one season of performances (Walsh's own full-length version of *Faust*) lost its Arts Council revenue funding in spring 1991 and decided to cease operations. The companies of Rosemary Butcher and Sue MacLennan have managed to sustain a precarious existence with little or no state funding, though both have benefitted from the various sponsorship schemes now offered by private businesses.*

Second Stride also fell a near victim to the funding axe in spring 1991, when its application for a project grant was refused. One of the reasons given was the fact that dance had become a less important element in its increasingly collaborative produc-

---

*Even three years ago no one could have predicted how vital sponsorship would become in the small-scale arts. The Digital Dance Awards, the Prudential Arts Awards and Barclays New Stages Awards have become a crucial source of money in the funding of new work. And while no one chooses to bite the hand that feeds them, this is a worrying situation. Firstly, private money depends both on goodwill and the financial security of individual businesses; secondly there's a pressure on even the smallest companies to market themselves so that they appeal to sponsors and judges. The early days of New Dance when choreographers felt relaxed about flopping in public, when what seemed of prime importance was the experimentation with new ideas, have unfortunately gone.

tions. The company was saved, however, when money was given from a new panel at the Council dealing specifically with multi-media work.

If the company's mixing of dance, theatre and opera caused problems for funding bodies, it did make for powerful (and controversial) theatre. In *Heaven Ablaze in his Breast* (1990) Spink and McDonald worked closely with the composer Judith Weir to create a dance-opera based on E. T. A. Hoffman's tale *The Sandman*. Typically, Second Stride's version highlighted the disturbing aspects of the plot – its nightmarish blurring of reality and hallucination. Typically too, it was a genuinely collaborative work. Not only was the action relayed equally through singing and movement, but some of the main roles were actually played by both a singer and a dancer.

In *Lives of the Great Poisoners* (1991) the balance tipped more towards opera. The piece told the stories of four of history's most notorious poisoners: Medea, Dr Crippen, Madame de Brinvilliers (an eighteenth-century aristocrat), and Thomas Midgley, the inventor of leaded petrol and CFC gases. With a text by playwright Caryl Churchill that ran from witty wordplay to painful tragedy, and a jazz-influenced score by Orlando Gough, the central roles in this work were all taken by singers. Sections of mime and dance did, however, give extra emotional and physical texture to the action, as in the Medea story, where the Princess of Corinth looked as if she were literally being danced to death by a 'chorus of poisons'.

One of the original founders of Second Stride, Siobhan Davies, re-formed her own company in 1988 after leaving London Contemporary Dance Theatre. Like many choreographers who choose not to work with a large repertory company, she felt the need to have a small core of dancers whom she knew well and with whom she could further develop her own language.

From the first pieces she made for this company in 1988 – *Wyoming*, to music by John Marc Gowans, and *White Man Sleeps*, with music by Kevin Volans – Davies's choreography showed a new fluidity and intimacy of style. Increasingly influenced by release technique, she explored the way in which deep impulses of movement could travel through the body, sometimes developing into jumps and large swinging movements of the limbs, but also focusing on small gestures close to the body.

Though her works did not tell a story as such, each dancer seemed to possess a strong personality and to form clear relationships with the others on stage. In *Wyoming*, for instance, Davies drew on the experience of her recent travels in America to suggest the vastness of the Wyoming landscape and the lives of people within it. The smallness and wariness of human beings placed in a vast natural landscape was expressed in a range of solos. Paul Douglas had a dance of stretchy balances that were constantly thrown off course; Gill Clarke hugged the ground in sensuous rolls before galloping across the stage in startled flight.

While Davies returned from America to achieve a new prominence in British dance, Michael Clark, having joined forces with the American choreographer Stephen Petronio, became less visible. He spent some time touring in the latter's piece *MiddleSex Gorge*, and at the time of writing, he and Petronio plan to make a new work which will be seen on both sides of the Atlantic.

Of the smaller scale companies, DV8, The Cholmondeleys and Yolande Snaith, have all increased their audience both in Britain and overseas, to become well-established on the dance scene. Lea Anderson also now works with The Cholmondeley's brother company, The Featherstonehaughs. The image of this all-male group is rather similar to a rock band, with the dancers sporting sharp haircuts and modishly baggy suits. The format of their performances is also something like a gig. They perform short dance numbers rather than extended 'works' and each piece is given a bantering introduction by the dancers themselves.

Anderson's choreography, like that for The Cholmondeleys, is based partly on stylised everyday movement, and through this the group is able to present both serious and jokey studies of a wide range of male behaviour. They may be tramps in one piece, soldiers in another, macho boxers in a third. They do a piece where they glide around the stage like 1950s lounge lizards, or skip sweetly together in an Irish jig.

Matthew Bourne (like Anderson, a graduate from the Laban Centre) co-founded the group Adventures in Motion Pictures in 1987. Originally a small-scale repertory company presenting works by Bourne, Jacob Marley and others, it has recently become a vehicle for Bourne's own stylish and witty brand of dance theatre. Typical is his *Town and Country* (1991) which takes an alternately satirical and nostalgic view of a now-defunct England. In the 'Town' section, a tweedy and imperious upper-class set take over a smart hotel. A flighty young man and woman are bathed and scoured by their maid and manservant (to the theme music from 'Desert Island Discs'); a pair of homosexuals join in a stiff and secretive duet to Noel Coward's *Dearest Love*; and there's a two-minute dance version of the film *Brief Encounter* in which two couples go through the same tentative, eye-dabbing dance of love and guilt.

In the 'Country' section, peasants do a clog dance (with sly references to Ashton's *La Fille mal gardée*), while the upper classes hunt, shoot and fish, or dance lyrical odes to the beauty of nature. Here Bourne extends the gestural base of his choreography to include neat springing footwork, strongly sculpted body shapes and inventively decorative arm movements.

Other new names that have emerged in recent years are the group Motionhouse, and the duet Mark Murphy and Sue Cox. The latter's choreography often displays the hard, dangerous edge seen in some Belgian and French new dance, while the former work in a softer style based on contact and release.

The question arises with all of this work though, whether the term 'New Dance' still has any relevant application. The influence of the movement can certainly still be seen, most importantly in the variety of styles and media with which today's choreographers feel free to work. Dance-makers continue to use film, speech, song and props as material, and more importantly continue to raid all forms of movement to extend their own language. Anderson's idiosyncratic gestural range, Snaith's fast, hard version of release, DV8's impassioned and dangerous use of manoeuvres developed out of contact improvisation – are all legacies from the ideas and experiments of the 1970s.

The effects of the New Dance movement can also be seen in the appearance of today's independent dancers, many of whom bear little resemblance to the physical stereotypes that used to dominate dance companies. There's nothing sylph-like about any of The Cholmondeleys or Snaith, while among The Featherstonehaughs, one dancer is a delicate five foot, and another reaches a startling six foot seven.

The kind of political thinking that activated so many of the dancers and choreographers associated with X6 is also evident in the work of companies like DV8. In its belief that pure dance is escapist and elitist, and its exploration of issues such as loneliness, aggression the oppression of women, and the alienation of gay men, DV8 is as concerned with 'making connections to the world' as were Claid, Lansley, and others.

Yet while for many other choreographers working today, such political issues are pressing, they are often handled with far less anger and bite. Matthew Bourne's *The Infernal Galop* (1990) presented a memorably poignant encounter between two gay men in a French *pissoir*, and showed how homosexual desire is fettered by the need for secrecy. Yet this was placed in a witty study of Parisian street life – whose jokes were sparked from satirising tourist clichés and from parodying styles in both life and dance. Equally, Jacob Marley's *Does Your Crimplene Go All Crusty When You Rub?* featured a cast of geriatrics and eccentrics that may have been a comment on ageist attitudes in dance. In fact the point was not to arouse sympathy, but to create a (hilarious) style where full-throttled dance was performed in a manner akin to late-stage Parkinson's disease.

The force of feminism has also noticeably abated. While Yolande Snaith's early work dealt subversively with images of women (Snaith dressed in a blousey pink corset, dragging a wardrobe around by chains) it has since moved towards a more broadly surreal vision. In *Court by the Tale* (1990) Snaith moved between images of the past, present and future, drawing the viewer into a maze of visual puns. Lea Anderson, too, will argue that the all-female composition of The Cholmondeleys is important to her because it allows her to avoid heterosexual dance clichés (different movements for men and for women, fixed ways of partnering, etc.). It also means that she can devote herself to portraying the behaviour of different types of women – the scatty ballerinas in *The Cholmondeley Sisters*, the obsessive saints and martyrs in *Flesh and Blood*. But her work is not overtly feminist – there are no messages about the condition of women, no analysis and no discernible anger on display, just the curiosity and wit of Anderson's imagination.

A further difference between early New Dance and present-day independent work is a new emphasis on image. Compared with the plain practice clothes and minimally staged works that dominated the 1970s, work in the late 1980s has tended to be very well and very fashionably dressed. Visual impact tends to be made as much by clothes, props, lighting and set as by move-ment, and often the designer's style seems to be as critically on show as the choreographer's.

There is, too, a general drift back to hard-core technique amongst the younger choreographers. Many are showing a renewed interest in more traditional vocabulary – beaten jumps, high extensions, fast, ground-covering steps, detailed rhythms, arabesque and attitude lines – as well as an interest in more com-plex compositional structures. Some choreographers, like David Massingham, have reverted quite straightforwardly to conven-tional dance values; others, like Jacob Marley, twist them to spectacularly bizarre effect – straight ballet steps are overlaid with bravura geriatric dodderings, and then complicated by details from Indian, disco or folk dance. Dancers themselves have had to become skilled in styles ranging from contact improvisation to ballet, Cunningham to T'ai Chi. And where sleekness, supple-ness, and brilliance of co-ordination used, in some quarters, to be considered slightly suspect display, they are now fully back in demand.

Fergus Early's statement in 1986 that 'the one and only con-cept essential to New Dance is liberation' may arguably have more relevance to the 1970s than to the early 1990s, at least from an aesthetic viewpoint. There was then a far greater divide between the establishment and experiment; radical approaches had a much greater power to shock; there were far fewer dancers and choreographers working independently of large companies, and thinking politically about dance was still a novel idea. New Dance then stood for all the liberating forces which helped to establish today's variety of small-scale independent dance.

Some writers now prefer to use the term 'post-modern dance' rather than 'New Dance' to describe the work of a number of choreographers working at present. The label is used in other art forms to describe work that mixes different styles and that jumbles up references to different kinds of art and culture. Jacob Marley and Matthew Bourne come to mind here, as does Michael Clark with his stylistic mix of classical ballet, Cunningham and punk, his use of Chopin, bagpipes and rock music, his borrowings from *Swan Lake* and the musical *Hair*.

Fashions in dance change fast – and it would be worrying if no one had moved on from the 1970s and the early 1980s. But there is one depressing factor that has partly influenced some of the developments in new dance – and that is the pressure placed on companies to woo their audiences and sponsors.

Choreographers like Lansley, Butcher and others certainly never had much money, but they did start working in a climate that allowed for a degree of public failure. They could be more interested in the ideas they were exploring than in worrying whether their audience would be irritated, bored, alienated or shocked. This doesn't mean that today's dance-makers don't experiment and don't believe in what they are doing. But they know that their work has to look good, that it has to have a certain polish, and that it has to have snappy publicity if it is to attract more bookings and more funding.

Yet the last few years have seen positive developments too. Against frightening financial odds, work of a high quality continues to be made, the language of dance continues to be expanded and audiences continue to grow. New Dance has also broken into television. In 1986 Channel 4 commissioned a television crew to work with Ian Spink, Siobhan Davies and a small group of dancers in order to find new ways of filming dance. Spink and Davies experimented with the freedom of location given them by the camera (Spink made one short piece in a derelict warehouse). They played with the ways in which different camera angles could affect the quality of the movement: a floor-to-ceiling shot that made an ordinary balance held on the edge of a small rostrum look like a suicidal lean over a precipice; a close-up could dramatically enlarge a small gesture or highlight a particular part of the body. They found how a moving camera could insert itself within a *pas de deux*, could gallop alongside a travelling step to make it seem even faster. They discovered how editing could create new rhythms, and give a different pace to their original phrases of dance.

Since this project, other directors and choreographers have become involved in the making of dance for television – either reworking existing pieces for the small screen, or making completely new works. As a result, DV8, The Cholmondeleys, Laurie Booth, Yolande Snaith, and Second Stride have all been seen on television, sometimes at prime viewing time. The Arts Council and the BBC have also commissioned a series of ten-minute dances made by a wide range of young choreographers and directors.

Television could become a very important source of money

and promotion for new work, and more importantly could bring dance to a much bigger audience than any live performance. The move from X6 to television may have taken fifteen years to accomplish, but it's an impressive one – and it's just one demonstration of how much energy and potential lay in those early experiments that rightly called themselves New Dance.

Appendix

A roll-call of new companies formed during 1970s shows how fast the independent dance scene expanded. As well as the various groups and soloists based around X6 there were:

In London

Another Dance Group. Directed by Nikolais-trained Sue Little and ex-London Contemporary Dance Theatre principal Ross MacKim. It was formed in 1972 and stopped operating around 1978.

Basic Space. An all-woman group who were mostly trained at London School of Contemporary Dance, directed by choreographer Shelley Lee. It was founded in 1976 and stopped operating c. 1986.

Cedar of Lebanon. A religious dance company founded by Janet Randell in 1974 which combined modern and medieval movement; no longer operating.

Extemporary Dance Company. Another Place-based group which was founded by Geoff Powell in the summer of 1975 to show works at the Edinburgh Fringe Festival and reformed in 1976. Later became Extemporary Dance Theatre under Emilyn Claid. Disbanded in 1991.

Junction Dance Company. Formed in 1976 by Kris Donovan and Ingegerd Lonnroth as a showcase for dancers and choreographers from The Place. It came to an end c. 1980.

MAAS Movers. The first all-black dance company, formed in 1978 to combine jazz and modern dance. Stopped operating in the early 1980s.

Moving Visions. Also formed by Ross MacKim and Sue Little. In 1978 Northern Arts and North-West Arts invited MacKim and Little to Darlington, and in 1982, the company, renamed English Dance Theatre, was taken over by Yair Vardi. In 1984 it moved to Newcastle and in 1988 was taken over by Jacky Lansley. Now disbanded.

Rosemary Butcher Dance Company. Formed in 1976, still operating.

Sally Cranfield and Judith Katz. Two more London School of Contemporary Dance graduates who made performance art pieces in unlikely environments, like a deserted house in Belgravia; worked during the late 1970s, but no longer together.

Strider. Formed by Richard Alston in 1972, it became Richard Alston and Dancers in 1977, and evolved into Second Stride in 1982.

Outside London

Cycles. Founded in 1974 by Cecilia McFarlane, and although based in Leamington Spa – receiving funds from the West Midlands Arts Association – it toured in schools, colleges, arts centres etc. all around Britain. It was formed with the intention of introducing a wide range of modern dance to audiences outside London, and its performances were always accompanied by classes and workshops.

EMMA Dance Company. Formed in 1976 by East Midlands Arts to provide the region with regular professional modern dance performances. In 1980 became New Midlands dance but stopped operating in 1988.

Janet Smith and Dancers. Formed in 1976 as a small-scale dance group in Leeds, performing Smith's own choreography. By 1982 it was a middle-scale company with repertoire including works by Robert North, Christopher Bruce and company members. Folded in 1988.

Ludus. Set up in 1975 as a dance-in-education group, initially with funds from the Arts Council but from 1978 with support from North-West Arts. Nearly all of the company's work has been done in schools, and their shows deal with subjects that are very much part of the children's lives. (See Note 2 below for a more detailed account of their methods.)

Moving Being. Founded in 1968 by Geoff Moore as a multi-media performance company. Moved form London to Cardiff in 1972.

Phoenix Dance Company. All-black, all-male dance group performing jazz/modern repertoire. Formed in Leeds in 1981. In 1990 took on women dancers.

Welsh Dance Theatre. Set up in 1975 by the American dancer and choreographer William Louther to perform modern dance classics by

Graham, Humphrey and others. The group was later re-formed into a collective presenting original choreography and Louther now runs his own company in London.

Note 1. From the mid-1970s onwards, growing numbers of Asian, African and Afro-Caribbean dance groups and artists began performing in Britain. In many ways, their struggle for funding and recognition parallels that of New Dance – but the dance forms are themselves too complex to be treated within the limits of this book.

Note 2. Ludus have developed a unique way of working with schools that has become something of a model. Their 'programmes' come in three parts: a performance of the work, a series of workshops and discussions led by members of the company, which follow up the theme of the performance, and finally the educational materials which are provided for the teachers. These include an advance pack of written material which helps the teacher to familiarise the children with the content of the show, and a follow-up pack which contains the music from the performance plus suggestions for movement lessons based on what the children have seen.

Emilyn Claid's review of *Big School* (*New Dance* 12, Autumn 1979 p. 6) describes a typical performance by the company. The piece was devised by Leslie Hutchinson, Chris Thomson, Kiki Gale, Laurie Booth and Jill Greystone. It was danced by Gale, Greystone and Booth and the music was by Roger Lewis.

> Stage set – a wasteground with an old push chair, a big chest, an old hat stand, barrels and various bits of rubbish.
>
> Julie enters and dances her way through playing with the objects . . . this areas is her 'den' . . . She wears a school uniform. 12 years old. Strong, energetic, ready for any sort of fun and game. Mandy joins her. Although also 12 years old she is quite different, the sophisticated type. Slight swing of the hips, slower walk, reading a magazine, full of airs and graces. These two are friends although Mandy never quite lets go . . . They play together, riding about in the push chair . . . Steven enters, and the girls hide . . . He acts younger than them, is 10 years old. . . . He plays with the objects, and has the quick nervous energy of a child in someone else's territory. Julie comes out to play with him, and they get to know each other by showing off their various skills and setting feats for each other. Mandy is . . . angry with Julie for playing with . . . a boy younger than herself. She grabs Steven's package . . . and opens it, revealing a new school blazer ready for his first term at the Big school. All is resolved when Steven produces a clown's nose . . . which surprises them all, and comes into his own with a display of

143

somersaults. Dance is the only performing skill used throughout and the story is told through the movements and facial expression of the dancers.

Claid goes on to describe the workshops and discussions which took place afterwards, where each group of children was led by a member of the company. At first the children talked about the issues which the piece raised, how they felt about changing schools and about children who were older or younger than themselves. Then Laurie Booth tried to get them to relate the idea of bullying to a more general theme of oppression. (Claid felt here that the children were not given enough chance to talk about themselves.) Afterwards there were movement workshops, which she describes as 'stretching, rolling, a bit of improvisation, running in slow motion, and games such as statues, where one person is put into a position by others in the group, who then get into a position around them. Never once were the boys made to feel silly, which I'm sure helped them to think positively about dance.'

Glossary

Trisha Brown
American choreographer, founder member of Judson Dance Theater (1962) and improvisational group Grand Union (1970). Many of her early works were made for extraordinary sites – taking place on rooftops, up the walls of buildings or suspended in nets. Others were built around strong formal structures such as *Line-Up* (1976–77) where all the movements were based around the instruction to get in line – or the 'accumulation' pieces (1971–72), where movements were added on and repeated in strict mathematical succession. Though Brown's earlier works tended to use very plain, functional movement, her most recent choreography has become more fluid and elaborate.

John Cage
American composer who has collaborated on numerous works with Merce Cunningham. His work explores different methods of composition, including chance methods and experiments with different kinds of technique, including electronically treated sounds and 'prepared' piano (i.e. a piano where objects have been placed on or between the strings to create a completely different noise). His *4' 33"* is the most famous piece of 'silent music' ever written.

Contact improvisation
This was developed in New York in 1972 by Steve Paxton and various student athletes and dancers. It is a form of duet in which the movement is invented by the dancers as they go along, the only rule being that the participants have to keep in close contact with the other's body. Any part of the body can be used to lean against, hang on to or balance on, and the movements can range from rolling over each other, lifting each other, to pushing, pulling, throwing and catching. By developing trust, agility, alertness and relaxation the dancers learn to follow where the movement takes them, how to go with their partner's momentum or how to change its direction.

People trying to describe contact improvisation have compared it with wrestling, martial arts, jitterbugging, gymnastics and the rough-and-tumbles of small children. It can be very slow, tender and exploratory, or very fast and athletic, and it is something in which both trained and untrained dancers can participate. It is exhilarating to do in workshops, and when you see those who are practised in the art, it also has the variety and excitement of any other dance form. Contact improvisation is of great interest to feminists because it teaches women how to lift and support men, and it involves no distinction of sexual roles.

Cunningham technique
A dance technique developed by Merce Cunningham from the late 1940s onwards. The style of movement is characterised by elements both from ballet (the vertical stance, the use of fast footwork and high leg extensions) and from modern dance (the curves and twists of the torso).

Cunningham also incorporates everyday movements into his dances, and often very quirky gestures. His movement phrases tend to be based on very complex rhythms, and may involve different parts of the body doing very different movements simultaneously. Unlike Graham, Cunningham does not believe that dance has to express anything but itself, and his works are often constructed out of very complex formal ideas. Certain elements, like the ordering of phrases, the number of dancers and so on, are frequently decided by chance (throwing coins etc.); another important feature of his work is the fact that dance, music and design are all composed independently of each other.

Feminism
In the 1970s the struggle for women's rights became very strong in Europe and America. Feminist arguments concerning the sexual, social, political and economic liberation of women became widespread, and did much to change the way in which men and women viewed themselves and each other.

Graham technique
A dance technique developed by Martha Graham from the late 1920s onwards. The style of movement is characterised by flexed feet and joints (as opposed to the long straight lines of ballet), by percussive movements of the torso, by movements performed on or close to the floor, and by stark, undecorated phrases of movement. Graham believed that all movement should be expressive of emotion, and that dance should relate to the drama and conflict of modern life. In later years, Graham's work became more fluid and lyrical, and a softer version of her style has formed the basis of much of London Contemporary Dance Theatre's repertoire.

Doris Humphrey
American choreographer who was also one of the great pioneers of modern dance. She thought of dance as existing between two 'deaths'

146

– the body lying prone, or standing firmly erect – both of which lack any kind of excitement. Dance happens through a process of fall and recovery when the body moves from these positions of stability, encounters gravity, defies it and then recovers its equilibrium.

Jasper Johns
Contemporary American painter associated with 'pop' art school.

Kathak
Dance form originating in North India, which combines Hindu and Muslim elements, dance and mime. Its special characteristics are its whipping turns and fast, rhythmic footwork.

Other dance forms from different parts of India also have their own very distinctive styles.

Minimalism
This term can be applied to all the arts, and refers to work which uses very ordinary materials arranged in very simple forms. Carl André's sculpture of bricks laid in straight lines is the most famous example in the visual arts. In music the term applies to compositions where a limited set of chords or sounds are repeated over and over again with a few basic variations. (In systems music, the variations are created in relation to strict mathematical systems.)

Minimalist choreography uses very plain movements – walking, rolling, running, simple gestures, etc. – that may follow very simple floor patterns like lines and circles. There is rarely any elaborate design and often no music; the interest and beauty of the dancing comes from the hypnotic effect of repetition, also from looking closely at the mechanics of ordinary movement and seeing images, patterns and details in it that we don't notice in everyday life.

Meredith Monk
American choreographer who began making work in the mid-1960s. Her pieces tend to cross categories, involving film, speech, props, song and dance; they are sometimes very long and often created for extraordinary venues. She has made works for lofts and parking lots, for a lake and for an opera house, and she often has her audience moving around so that they see the work from different places and from different angles (parts of *Vessel* (1971) were seen by the audience through windows).

Performance art
Performance art was originally developed by visual artists (i.e. people trained in painting, sculpture, design etc.) who became interested in

147

using themselves as the raw material for their work. A wide variety of 'events' came under its label – continuous recitals of songs, lying in a bath for days on end, arranging and manipulating various props to create extraordinary visual images. Some events were like exhibitions, to which people could come and go; others were scheduled performances.

Performance art has now become a loose term for any kind of highly visual live performance that may use, but does does not come under the strict heading of dance, drama, film, music or mime; and for work where the ideas and images involved follow a strange, sometimes hallucinatory logic.

Physical theatre
This is another loose term which describes any kind of theatrical performance where the use of movement and gesture is more important than words, but where no strict dance or mime technique is involved.

Post-modern
This is often used loosely to describe experimental art from the 1960s onwards, but it is more strictly applied to any art which challenges traditional definitions of itself. This challenge may either come from using a variety of different styles within a single work (the term was first coined to describe buildings that employed an eclectic mix of architectural styles) or by mixing different art forms. In dance the term usually refers to choreography which doesn't follow a strict technique, but may employ everyday movement, martial arts, contact etc.; and to performances that may involve dance, film, acting, singing, manipulation of props and so on. The other characteristic of post-modern work is that it rarely has an obvious storyline or logical progression: dancers may take on different characters, as in *Bösendorfer Waltzes* or Laurie Booth's *Animal Parts*; objects may stand for one thing and then another; snatches of music may give way to speech and then to film; and the dancing itself may often be disrupted by other kinds of activity.

'Post-modern' is a term that clearly applies to most of the work associated with the New Dance movement, although post-modernism does not necessarily embrace the political views that were central to the evolution of New Dance.

Project grant
Funds given by the Arts Council to support individual works or choreographic projects.

Yvonne Rainer
American choreographer, and founder member of Judson Dance Theater. She used simple tasks and non-dance movement in works that

were often open-ended, i.e. parts could be interchanged or inserted into other dances. She is best known for the ongoing *Trio A* (1966–68), and for her minimalist manifesto in which she declared an end to 'spectacle' and 'virtuosity' in dance. Now works with film.

Release

Popularly described as dancing 'from the inside out', release involves a strong awareness of the body's internal structure. Starting from a period of quiet stillness and concentration, the dancer tries to become fully conscious of the state of his or her body: the way the bones are joined together, the state of tension and relaxation in the muscles, the way the limbs rotate in the joints, the way the weight is distributed, whether it is in a state of balance or imbalance and so on. As the dancer moves around he or she then tries to find the most relaxed and natural positions of the body, and the most economical and comfortable ways of moving: making sure that there is no unnecessary tension in the muscles, avoiding bad postural habits, checking that the movement is working naturally with the breathing.

Often dancers work with mental images which help them to sense the body more clearly, for example rather than being told simply to 'pull up' or 'stand up straight' – instructions that might immediately make the dancers tense up and hold themselves badly – the dancers may think in terms of a line running through the centre of the body and up through the head, a line which forms the centre of balance around which the body moves, and along which the body lengthens. Or they may think of the weight falling down the back and lifting up through the front as way of balancing the body.

Dancers working with release tend to look soft and relaxed when they move, though this does not have to be the case. Very fast and very hard movement can be performed with the dancer still focusing on the natural line of the body, the placing of the weight, the breath, the releasing of *unnecessary* tension.

Revenue funding

Funds given by the Arts Council to companies, artists or organisations on a yearly basis.

Frank Stella

Contemporary American painter, works with geometrical abstract patterns in bright colours.

Surrealists

Group of writers and visual artists during the 1920s and 1930s who tried to express the subconscious in their work. Among their favourite techniques were recreating dreams and hallucinations and practising automatic writing. Famous names include Salvador Dali, René Magritte and André Breton.

T'ai Chi Chuan
A Chinese form of martial arts which is practised in both East and West as a form of movement meditation. Movements are slow and sustained, closely co-ordinated with the breathing, and the weight is heavily grounded.

Bibliography

Much of the source material for this book has come from interviews, old programmes, unpublished Arts Council reports and my own notes. The main published sources are the magazines:

Time Out
New Dance
Dance Theatre Journal

Other useful works of reference:

Banes, S. *Terpsichore in Sneakers: Post-Modern Dance* (2nd edn, Middletown, Conn.: Wesleyan University Press, 1987).
For an account of American post-modern dance.

Jordan, S. *Striding Out: Aspects of Contemporary and New Dance in Britain* (London: Dance Books, 1992).

McDonagh, D. *The Rise and Fall and Rise of Modern Dance* (2nd edn, London: Dance Books, 1990).

Novak, C. *Sharing the Dance: Contact Improvisation and American Culture* (Madison, Wisc.: University of Wisconsin Press, 1990).

Tufnell, M. and Crickmay, C. *Body Space Image* (London: Virago, 1990).

White, J. (ed.) *Twentieth Century Dance in Britain: A History of Five Dance Companies* (London: Dance Books, 1985).
For history of main ballet and modern companies.

Index

Pages including illustrations are shown in *italic*.

Printed in the United Kingdom
by Lightning Source UK Ltd.
133347UK00001B/403-444/A